PROSTITUTION
TO PREACHING

PROSTITUTION TO PREACHING

FREEDOM IS POSSIBLE

STAN MONS

REDEMPTION
PRESS

Published by Redemption Press, 70 S. Val Vista Drive, Suite A3-442, Gilbert, AZ 85296.

Redemption Press is honored to present this title in partnership with the author. The views expressed or implied in this work are those of the author. Redemption Press provides our imprint seal representing design excellence, creative content, and high-quality production.

All Scripture quotations in this publication are taken from the New King James Version® (NKJV). Copyright © 1982 by Thomas Nelson. Used by permission. All rights reserved.

ISBN 13: 978-1-64645-926-1 (paperback)
978-1-64645-927-8 (ePub)

Library of Congress Catalog Card Number: 2025906215

In memory of Nancy Verrall Warren

Whose love for Jesus and servant's heart left a lasting impression on me and this book.

—*Stan Mons*

CONTENTS

FOREWORD

I first met Stan Mons in 2012 when he arrived as a student at Summit International School of Ministry. I instantly recognized him as a totally unique individual, and the longer I know him, the more convinced I am that this is true.

Hailing from the Netherlands, Stan arrived at our Bible school with a remarkable testimony. As a young man in the shipyard industry, he had been ensnared in destructive life patterns until a transformative encounter with Jesus changed the course of his life forever.

I could see early on that Stan was not churched but was totally sold out for Jesus; he brought an inspiring freshness and boldness to his approach to reaching others. After graduation, he served in different areas; organizing impactful youth conferences in Norway, ministering as an intern in Canada, and co-pastoring in Maine. In 2014, he found the love of his life in Inna, and together, they embraced a calling that led them to establish Safe House Church in Portland, Oregon, a place where lives are being transformed through God's love.

As young as Stan is, he has shared something timeless in this book. His story takes us on a journey of the tragedies and triumphs of the human heart. In moments of vulnerability, Stan shares his story with clarity and conviction that will not fail to move and inspire our faith.

This book is more than a mere collection of stories, it is a powerful testimony that deserves to be read and shared with others. It delves into the depths of the human experience, inviting us to embrace our vulnerabilities and discover the transformative power of the enduring love of Christ.

Scripture says, "In His light, we see light" (Psalm 36:9), meaning the Lord illuminates our understanding, giving us the power to see and perceive more than we thought possible. Stan's story gives us a similar seeing and understanding of the redemptive human experience found in Jesus.

Physically, Stan has notably bright blue eyes. With this book, may his bright spiritual eyes cause us to glimpse into our own stories through the eyes of God. His story inspires us to an ever-deepening commitment to heart and mind transformation through Jesus Christ. God bless Stan Mons, an incredibly unique individual, for writing this powerful book.

—Dr. Teresa Conlon, President,
Summit International School of Ministry
(the Bible School of Times Square Church, NYC)

CHAPTER 1

PRAYING TO SATAN

I was born and raised in the Netherlands, a small country in Europe. I never thought that I would leave my nation, neither did I ever plan for the way I live now. The first twenty-two years of my life were spent at home, and then God showed up.

Everyone on my mother's side of the family was well off and seemed so successful to me. Because my dad had married into this family, he strived continuously to try to create the lifestyle he thought we needed. He put in long hours, but no matter how hard my dad worked, he was never able to match the lifestyle and renown that my mom's side of the family enjoyed.

Watching my dad year after year, I ended up subconsciously feeling that there was more value in my mom's last name than in the one I carried. I grew up wanting my mom's last name and all that seemed to come with it. I wanted to be a part of their journey and their apparent success, which always felt slightly out of reach for me.

It seemed like my dad could not measure up, which left me wondering what life might have been like if he and I did not have the "wrong" last name. Would we have had more success and more wealth? As these feelings and emotions became ingrained in my identity, a seed of insecurity was planted.

While I was growing up, family was always important to me. I loved spending time with them, especially during the holidays. I always looked forward to the family days and events. All my aunts, uncles, and cousins would come together. We'd play games, have a great family meal, and go for long walks. Those days seemed to be much longer than the others. I felt more alive, and before the day was even over, I longed for the next visit. Every year, these were the times I cherished most.

As the insecurity continued to develop in my life, it somehow became harder to fully enjoy these times with my family. Thoughts slowly but surely began to consume my mind and started to affect my actions. I wondered, *Am I important to them? Am I wanted? Am I needed?*

I began to shut down. I did not want to deal with these thoughts. I worked hard like my dad, but no matter what I did I always felt like I was on the sidelines. I felt powerless and alone; like I was part of the family, yet I was eventually going to be left out.

I looked out the window of my room and thought, *I feel safe here.*

The ceiling and two of the walls were completely covered with ornate wood. The wood was nice and rather dark, but not too dark, so I was able to see the knots and flames. It looked as if someone had painted it. I never got tired of looking at it, just by myself, alone. That was when I would imagine something terrible happening to me.

What would it be like if …? Would they cry for me? Would they miss me? In my mind I see it so clearly, they are all standing at my grave. They would cry … no, really cry. I finally see in their teary eyes that they love me and miss me, that I am special to them, that they care. I can see that it finally hits them—they are realizing they do really care for me. I feel warm, pleasant. Will death make me feel this good, this loved?

I thought about it often, alone in my room, looking at my ceiling.

One night, as I longed to find out if I was loved, the idea of committing suicide began to make sense to me. I wondered if I would even be missed. How often would they think of me? *They will probably love and think of me more if I am dead. They will realize that I was needed; maybe that is the way? Maybe ...*

Then my mom called, "Dinner is ready."

I ran down with my emotional mask on, pretending I was normal and all right.

"How was your day?" Mom asked.

"My day was fine, Mom."

Without looking up, she fired off the follow-up question, "Any grades?"

I could not deal with the possibility of being a disappointment, so I responded, "I believe I had one B plus."

I lied. Often when I would share my grades, the way my parents responded made me feel like I was a failure. When I would hear their response, it always made me feel that the right grade was somewhere hidden in the future. The one that I had come home with that day was definitely not it.

I was not sure if I would ever be able to bring home the grades that would make me feel loved and cherished by my parents. Since I did not like the feelings that their response to my grades would give me, lying helped.

I could lie the grades away or lie them higher. It was easier to lie and avoid the bad feelings than to go through them, at least for that day.

Lying was so much easier, especially for me. That was the only way I had learned to not get hurt while I tried to figure out how to be loved. If I could only change who I was, then I could be myself and be loved at the same time; but not yet. That day, lying was safer.

At the end of dinner, Mom said to me, "After we read the Bible at the table, please help clear the dishes."

"It's his turn." I pointed at my little brother.

"I asked you …" Mom raised a stern brow at me. "Didn't I?"

I swallowed hard. "Okay, Mom."

Finally, back in my room alone, everything made sense to me. I knew what to do. *This could be the change I need; this can change the course of my life. They will love me; they will respect me. They will want to be a part of my life!*

***

All those years growing up, my parents took me to church. Church was nonnegotiable. It was part of our normal routine, something we just did. Hearing about God and the stories of the Bible was awesome, and I could see them play out in my imagination.

But life—all the fitting in I had to do and hiding my desires for fun, pretending they weren't in my heart—got me frustrated. This wasn't the cool life I imagined after hearing the Sunday school Bible stories. It was boring and uneventful. By the time I was twelve years old, I had realized I had to take control if I wanted success and a meaningful life; if I wanted to achieve something, to be somebody.

I was taught that praying to God was the right thing to do. In the Bible stories it seemed to work, but we lived in our time. As a kid, it felt like we were here on earth and God had retired to Heaven and that only some of the extraordinarily good people from church would one day join Him there.

I needed someone to help me get the life I needed sooner than "one day"; to be the man I dreamed about becoming—a man who was respected, loved, and valued.

This God of my parents did not seem to hear me, and I wasn't strong or good enough to expect much help from Him anyway. I needed something else, someone else.

From the things I'd overheard friends bragging about, I knew there was another way. I took a deep breath …

I need cardboard, a marker, and a glass.

My adrenaline pumped as I ran through the house gathering all my materials. Quickly, I made a homemade Ouija board. I placed the glass on it, along with my finger. My heart was pumping in my throat. I took one more deep breath …

"Devil, will I be rich?"

Nothing.

"Devil, will I be successful?"

Nothing.

I waited, then I positioned myself in front of my desk, knelt, and started praying to Satan, at first timidly, but eventually challenging him from the depths of my soul. It was frightening, and in a scary way, exciting.

I finally said, "If you make me rich and successful, you can have my soul."

I felt cold and alone. Why did Satan not respond to me in a big, impressive way? I had heard and believed the stories my friends told me about witchcraft and calling on spirits. I had decided to trust the Devil and acted in faith that he would respond to me.

Why was there no movement on my Ouija board? Does even Satan not want me?

Soon, I found out that something *did* happen and change; a spiritual door into my life was now open to Satan.

A string of bondage had been tangled skillfully around my neck, and quietly, Satan would wait for the opportune moments to add more strings, year after year.

CHAPTER 2

OUT OF CONTROL

During my teenage years, I started dating someone I shouldn't have. By the time I began to realize how much dating her was changing and destroying who I was, it was too late; I was in too deep.

I thought it was going to be great when we began to date.

Right off the bat I told her, "I go to church. I don't want to sleep with anyone before marriage."

She did not have a problem with this and even seemed open to going to church. That was something I needed her to do to make this work without risking damage to my relationship with my family. I had heard warning after warning against getting close to a girl who does not go to church... but what if you like her?

Despite presenting my boundaries upfront, it was not long before we got physical. Only weeks after we started dating, all those boundaries were broken and soon forgotten. At that time, I still didn't really know her at all and had no clue what I had gotten myself into.

Because of overstepping the boundaries, our connection changed dramatically. I felt bound to her, like something irreversible had been put into motion and now I had to stay with her, to see it through. *I have to make it work with her.*

I felt like I had failed God and my family by breaking all boundaries. *Maybe seeing the relationship through till the end, eventually marriage, could in a way kind of fix this wrong.*

I felt obligated, determined to make it work. *I cannot become the black sheep of the family.*

Quickly I began to get to know her better, and what I saw was not pretty. She was a compulsive liar. Stories about what she had done over the weekend, or any other time, often simply did not add up. Her parents, her friends, and I would all get different versions of her stories.

The hardest part was that many times there seemed to be no reason to lie. As far as I could understand, I saw nothing that needed to be covered up. Yet without fail, there were always new stories. It started to affect me, but I could not allow it to be a problem. I had to hope, I had to trust, and I had to swallow it all so we could continue dating!

I put the concerns aside time after time and tried to set sail, hoping that somehow we would end up in better waters. Every time I hoped, I would end up disappointed. I would always choose to give my trust again, yet she would always break it.

I started to notice anxiety; I had never really dealt with that before. Strange things were happening, and my feelings, emotions, and responses were changing. I was changing.

I never knew what was going to come next, what was true, or what would prove to be a lie. Soon, even trying to figure out what was true or made up just became so painful; all outcomes felt dangerous. *If she speaks the truth and I question her, I may hurt her feelings. We may end up in a fight. If she is lying but I trust her, I may be disappointed and hurt again.*

Every word could become my next disappointment; every action could be the next breach of the trust I was so willing to give.

I began to feel tired, hurting constantly. The one person I tried to talk with and be close to was the one who was causing most, if not all, of the hurt. But I couldn't leave.

I could not become the black sheep of the family. I had seen it before, the way people talked about and treated a young couple after they broke up and it came out that they had slept together. They were marked as damaged goods and labeled as a failure. I saw these couples try to look good for everyone watching, seeking another way to somehow make up for their sin. They sought to be wholeheartedly welcomed back into the "good people" circle but were never really accepted or treated as if all had been erased.

I never saw anyone finish paying off the sin debt that was imposed on them by the community. It had separated them; no longer were they part of the talkers, they had become the talked about. This small group, separated by their found-out sins, seemed to have a lifelong membership. The talkers were always safe from being talked about, but a sin like sleeping around coming to light would guarantee your enlistment among that small but ever-growing group of outcasts. That could not happen to me. I would not become an outcast to my family.

Since we had slept together, I could not break up with the girl I was now supposed to marry. That was the only way

I thought I could fix all this. *I had to make it work. I will force it to work!*

For months, I begged and pleaded with her in secret. I tried to talk to her. I chose to be vulnerable, to be forgiving. Numerous times I wept in the arms that were hurting me. But month after month I stayed the course, even though I was breaking.

I had given myself on all levels—all my strength, heart, body, and efforts. Every choice I made to make this work took me deeper. So deep, I was stuck in a place where I got hurt more and more, to the point of panic, constant fear, and pain. As I changed, I became more desperate. *I must make this work.*

The pain and burden were outgrowing me. Carrying this alone and having to hide our issues any time I came around people who loved me was wearing me out. I quickly grew exhausted.

I felt no control over when and how I would be hurt next. It began to control me. I was being filled with fear and started to have panic attacks. *I need to take control of the pain and disappointments.*

Slowly but surely, I became manipulative. I did not want to, but I felt so much fear and anger inside. It felt like it was ripping me apart, like it was trying to kill me. I had an impossible task at hand. I had to fight—fight for survival—and not lose the relationship in the process.

While fear and panic grew, they began to influence my decisions. At any given time when the fear of being hurt or lied to struck, I wanted to know where she was and what she was doing, and I needed a way to verify it. As the hurt started to control me, my need to control our situation, and ultimately her, kept growing.

Whenever the demands of my fears were not met, if she didn't pick up the phone or respond to my texts, or if things just seemed like they were not panning out, immediately panic would strike me. I'd see myself transform instantly, as if I had developed two personalities. One moment I'd be fine, and in an instant I became mean, driven, and unreasonable. I couldn't sleep, rest, or focus until I had a grip on the situation again.

Unfortunately, I often found out that her secret actions were far beyond my greatest fears. All of this kept fueling my pain and brokenness, month after month. I kept giving it my all, but it was just not enough. All I had left in me was deep, deep pain and fear.

All this time, my parents had been watching me from the sidelines. There was no way I could truly hide it all from them. They saw me literally deteriorate and lose my joy. They tried to say something from time to time, but none of that mattered to me. I could not let them get through to me. Breaking off my relationship was simply not an option, so I could not even consider their comments. I had to deny what was going on so I had a shot at making it all work in the future. I had to.

One evening, however, it was different. My dad came into my room, and my mom stood in the doorway.

My father sat down on the bed, his eyes filled with worry. "How are you doing?"

Clearly they had planned this intervention, but since I had been kept out of the loop, I had to think on my feet. *What do they know? Which of my secrets needs defense?*

I just shrugged and tried to ignore them. I hoped my apparent unwillingness to cooperate would deflect further confrontation, but instead of leaving me be, my dad began to voice his genuine concern about my girlfriend and her effect on my wellbeing. He must have realized I wasn't listening, because he leaned in and pushed harder.

"She is not good for you. I'm seeing my own child change for the worse, and I'm not going to just stand by and let it happen."

Something registered in me as those words left my dad's mouth. *My dad is a threat to the relationship.* In a split second, I exploded, my swinging fists coming down on my father. He tried to avoid them, grabbed me around my waist, and ran me into furniture. I pounded away on his back and head.

Mom was screaming in the doorway. "You guys are killing each other! *No!*"

My little brother came running. The fight broke off, and everyone stood there, stunned and quiet. I was furious. I was caught off guard by my anger but more determined than ever to make my relationship work, with or without my family. Fear, panic, and hurt had transformed me and filled me with anger and a need to be in control … always.

CHAPTER 3

A BIG BLACK EMPTY HOLE

I waved at my girlfriend, signaling her to get in the car. We were going on a date.

A good friend and I had recently moved my girlfriend into her own apartment. I really hoped that having her own place would help her leave some turmoil behind. I thought some of it was being caused, or at least amplified, by her parents' divorce. Even though this move would not solve any of the lying, I still hoped that somehow it would improve our situation.

I felt that little bit of hope so clearly, but as she got into the car, her phone pinged. In just that split second, I thought

I saw a glance of worry on her face. As I thought about it, the fear started to flare up, so I just said it …

"Hey, as you got that text, I looked for some response on your face. It's probably just me, but would you mind showing me that text, so I know I have nothing to worry about?"

"Really?" She snapped back. "You're going to check my phone again?"

I did my best to stay calm. "I just thought I saw a flash of worry when you got that text. Just show me so I know it's nothing."

Again, this transformation started to come over me. I couldn't help it. I was so damaged, so eaten up by fear and hurt, that I had to take control of the situation. I had to.

The fight started, going back and forth until we were both yelling, red hot with anger. It's hard to say how long it lasted. The whole time she had her phone clutched in her hand as the words flew back and forth.

Suddenly, she snapped. She got out of the car and threw her phone on the passenger seat, then slammed the door. I picked up the phone and started reading the conversation, as the texts revealed the secret relationship that had been going on behind my back. My heart froze in panic.

Everything slowed down. It seemed there was an eternity between my heartbeats as every word I read ripped open my soul to let the last drops of hope spill out on the floor mats of my car.

I could hardly breathe. My brain ran at lightning speed trying to find a way out, but there was none. I started to come back to the reality of my situation—panic, despair, survival. All I could think was, *Try! Just try!*

I swung open the passenger door as I held her phone. "Come in, come in, please come in."

She sat down.

"I will forgive you." My voice shook. "I don't mind what you have with him. Please stay with me. Please don't give up on what we have. I forgive you. I forgive you."

The fear overwhelmed me, and I started to weep as I begged her, realizing that none of it seemed to matter to her anymore. I could tell her heart was closing. She kept saying, "I don't know, Stan. I don't know," every time I asked about how we would go forward.

Eventually, without saying another word, she got out of the car. I drove off, not knowing what to do anymore.

***

Alone in my room, I tried to gather my thoughts. Instead of figuring it out, I became overwhelmed by the hurt and the betrayal. I had nothing left to give, no matter how deeply I sought within myself; there was nothing there that I had not already given away. I had nothing but the constant disappointment, the ever-growing reward of pain no matter what I had done. I felt broken, like I was dying from the inside out. With tears in my eyes, I made the hardest decision I had ever made up until that point. *I need to save myself. I need to survive.*

It felt like choosing life or choosing her. I felt like I was drowning, being weighed down so heavily by it all that I could not stay afloat any longer. I was gasping for air, and in a reflex of survival I called her and broke it off.

***

It had been about two weeks when my phone rang. An adrenaline rush got my heart pounding as I read her name on the screen, and gasping for air, I picked up the phone. Right away, she started telling me how much she missed me and how she needed me back.

Suddenly, the call was disconnected … or so I thought. For about ten minutes, I waited for her to call back, not wanting to mess up this moment.

What if …? What if she learned from all this? What if this is it?

She has realized that she cares for me, that she wants to be with me, that she needs me!

I felt a little hope again.

I picked up the phone and called her back. She answered, but I got cut off right away by a voice I did not know.

A woman's voice said, "Stop calling my brother's girlfriend, you stalker. She doesn't want you anymore. Just leave her alone like she wants you to."

With a brick in my stomach, I said, "Be careful. You have no idea who she is."

We never spoke again.

***

I looked up. It was only a few weeks later, and I enjoyed feeling the warm summer wind mixed with sunlight on my face. But something wasn't right.

All my life I had spent my summer vacations here. This harbor had become for me and many of my friends our second home. In a strange but very pleasant way, we had grown so close over the years. All of us were young adults with similar upbringings. We had amazing adventures, partying and enjoying an extravagant lifestyle.

I stood outside, overlooking the harbor, while most of my friends were already somewhere inside the small and exclusive club for us harbor kids. I tried to take in all that wealth tied up at the docks right in front of me. I thought of my parents and family somewhere on one of these yachts all together having a great time. I listened to my own breath as I took one more look. It was so clear. I wanted to care for my friends. I used to be grateful for enjoying all this wealth. I wanted to feel something for my family, but I was broken; there was just nothing left. I felt nothing anymore, just this big black empty hole with nothing in it.

The ring she had given me early on in our dating weighed strangely heavy in my pocket as I walked toward one of the far-left maintenance docks. It was quite a walk to get there. When I got to the end of the dock, I took out my knife. Slowly, I removed the ring from my pocket. Taking my time,

I used the last sunlight of the day to carve deep into that ring: *Trust Kills*.

As the sun disappeared, I threw the ring as far as I could. Once it hit the dark water, I vowed to never, ever trust again.

Turning around to walk back to the club, I muttered to myself, "I need a drink."

As the sunlight faded, a shiver went up my spine. It got colder quickly, but it was more than that. I was strangely aware of it. It seemed I had walked into a coldness caused by more than just the sun disappearing.

CHAPTER 4

WHAT DO I NEED?

I had finished college; finally, graduation was behind me. During a college internship, I had gotten to work in the design world within the super yacht industry. During this time, some of my assignments had been sent to clients without much need of adjustment. One client was so impressed that before long they offered me a full-time position. Full of excitement, I accepted, and right out of college I became head of design for a new yacht-development company.

At nineteen years old, I was making a great salary; the design work gave validity to this young company and allowed us to do better and open more doors than most.

The owner started to trust me, and I no longer had to work set hours. He instructed me to, "Just do whatever you need to do so you can keep delivering this kind of work."

I came and left when I wanted. I was good at what I did, and I enjoyed it. All seemed to be working out for me. I absolutely loved my job and living my childhood dream.

When I wasn't working, I spent my money and partied. Over time, it grew into an extreme—partying more and harder; drinking more and more often.

With that lifestyle came many shallow relationships that never really satisfied at all. I could not trust or connect with anyone on an emotional level. I would simply not allow anything or anyone into my life that could possibly hurt me; I tried to do damage control on my insides.

After some time, it had become normal that I would drink until I passed out, sometimes multiple times a week.

I threw money wherever I wanted, but I did it very strategically so things looked good on the outside for my friends and family. Working hard to make my life seem as impressive as possible had a consequence. My pain and hurts were being covered, not healed.

Quickly, I started losing all ability to really connect with people. I began to drift and separate more from the people who loved me and cared for me. It happened quickly, yet in a covert way so that it did not draw too much attention.

I loved partying and finding girls to spend some time with. I loved talking to girls. Nothing else could make me feel that way, but every time a girl would tell me she liked me or even loved me, I had to run! I could not be close to someone like that or have feelings for them. Not after what had happened in my first real long-term relationship. No more trust, no more threats.

People, and a real connection to them, had become a threat to me. I could not let them get close to me; I just wanted no more hurt. Of course I wanted to be loved, but I could not go down the road of trust again.

***

I remember the day.

Still with the same company, I was working in my office alone when the thought hit me:

I do not need an emotional connection. I don't need a relationship. I don't even want one. I do not need to risk the pain.

All I want, and all I need, I can get from prostitutes. They will not be a threat; I can talk about what I want and never see them again. I can be whoever I want to be. They will never hurt me or reject me. I will not have to trust. All I need is my money, and that I have.

Strangely enough, it wasn't hard for me to get into that kind of extreme life at all. It made perfect sense to me, and it quickly became a part of my life that grew steadily. There were many dangerous sides to it, but even though I was taking extreme risks in exploring the world of prostitution, I felt it was a safe place, a place of acceptance. It helped me avoid the possibility of rejection and pain.

Meanwhile, my drinking got worse. I was running fast, putting all my effort into this secret life that I believed would provide what I needed to fill that horrible hole in my heart. But with all I had now—success, money, respect, and sex—I still felt exactly the same.

Nothing.

***

Drinking began to become a problem. I got so used to the effects of alcohol that I needed more and more. I could not physically drink enough anymore to get the same high.

I just wanted to feel happy for a moment. I needed to get rid of that big black empty hole inside of me.

I needed to resort to stronger liquor to achieve the results I sought. In my head, however, I had a plan. *This is only temporary until I find the solution. I promise I'm figuring it out. I just need a break for now.* The liquor would give me a break from having to deal with my reality. I was paying a price though, and it began to show.

It became harder to hide the drinking. I would have so much alcohol in my system that when I woke up in the morning, I'd still be heavily drunk. Living a religious life and pursuing a high-level professional life, I couldn't have people notice my inability to control my drinking. *I will hide it better; I have to.*

As I put my mind to it, I got good at developing a double life. I knew and practiced giving all the right answers, trying to be quicker with words than anyone around me so I could stay ahead of the questions and silence people by intimidation. I had to keep a close watch on my timelines, always coming up with the right and fitting story or making up untraceable business appointments. It was important to explain away all the time lost to running with the prostitutes, my flings, and the drinking.

Ultimately, what seemed to work best for me was to manipulate people into feeling guilty about their own questions before they would even ask them. I reasoned; *I need to protect my secret life from any threat. This life leaves me in control. It will keep me from getting hurt and is soothing to my pain. Anything that contributes to the possibility of losing this life, all threats, need to be eliminated. No vulnerable relationships, not even with friends … no more weaknesses. If no one really knows me or anything about my secret life, then no one will try to take it from me. I must protect it. I need this life. The dark will let me keep it hidden. No more light …*

CHAPTER 5

A WAY OUT?

E ven though I was young, I had a very well-paying job at the company. When we hit the financial crisis of 2008, things began to change. Eventually, my employer offered a choice—leave the company or stay on without pay. I was promised that the company would accumulate paycheck-related debt toward me that they would make good on once they made it through the financial bad weather.

Growing up in a business family, I understood that staying on and having the company indebted to me could provide a very favorable future for me if the company made it in the long run. At that point, I still lived with my parents, so I had almost no financial responsibilities and had enough in the bank to take this risk.

I decided to stay on. Because of my commitment to the company, I gradually got more involved when bigger decisions needed to be made. Over the next few months, we didn't always agree on how to bring the company forward in a way that would bring us back into the black..

Over time, I noticed that I felt less and less appreciated due to having no pay and not seeing a return on my work. On top of that, the cost of my extreme lifestyle quickly ate away at my savings. By the time I was down to the last of my savings, I made my next decision.

My boss and I sat down and did all the paperwork on what the company owed me and how they would pay me back in the future. We signed agreements on the patents that I was involved in. I gave my resignation, and with my last savings, I started my own yacht-development company.

A company I had worked for during my last college internship had told me they would send work my way if I ever started for myself in the yachting industry. Hoping they would come through, I reached out. Almost instantly, they sent the first jobs my way, helping me get my company up and running. The projects I was involved in quickly got my name out there.

Because the company I had worked with was renowned in the yacht-building world, their open endorsement of my work got me noticed. My name-credit in the small and competitive world of yacht design began to build up. This helped me score my own projects, and soon I moved my company into an office building. It all seemed to just fall into place. I enjoyed my work so much that it never felt like a burden. The dream I'd had since being a teenager had now become reality. I owned my own yacht-development company.

***

My parents were well off, and there was no reason for me to move out yet. This put me in the position where I could spend all my money on whatever I wanted. It fed the party-and-prostitute lifestyle I was living, allowing me to run after whatever drew me to that world. I was making and spending more than ever before.

No one knew about my secret life or to what extreme I was living it. I had made up my mind that I wanted to keep it that way. Since the relationship that had destroyed me, I'd had many flings and over a dozen girlfriends. By that time, I had even more reasons to stay away from anything long-term, but not one of the girls I had been around in that time had impacted me the way this new girl would.

When I saw her for the first time, I thought, *She is so beautiful. If I get her, I won't need to run with the prostitutes anymore. She even goes to church. She is my way out.*

We started talking a little on and off but didn't start dating until we ended up at the same summer vacation spot. She opened the relationship with almost the exact same words I had spoken years earlier in what seemed like a long-forgotten memory: "I go to church. I don't want to sleep with anyone before marriage."

I answered, "Of course not!"

All the strings of bondage and darkness came with me into her life unannounced. She was not ready to deal with the level of darkness and the powers that were lording over my life, nor did I understand them at the time. It did not take long before all boundaries were neglected, broken, and forgotten.

***

Two weeks into the relationship, I found myself looking at the ceiling of a nice hotel room, thinking to myself, *Why am I here? The girl in the shower is not as attractive to me as my girlfriend; my girl is all I have ever sought after and yet I go through all this trouble to be here and make this meeting happen—why? It doesn't make sense. I thought for sure that my girl would be my way out of this life. Why am I here? There is something else going on. What gets me out here? It doesn't make sense that I am here when I have her back at home.*

For a few more moments I wondered, then I dropped it.

Nothing changed for the better. Nothing improved. *How in the world is she not the solution to the crazy life I'm living?* I had to lie even more now.

We had some good times together, but most of it was rough. With money and a lot of effort, we managed to make our relationship look decent on the outside, but we argued almost every moment when no one was looking.

Because of all my hurts, bondage, and darkness, I was very controlling and suspicious. I was constantly managing our relationship to avoid getting hurt ever again. Somewhere down the road, I started to manage her life to avoid having to deal with anything unexpected. I had to know everything— where she was, who she was with, why she was there, and how long she would be there. I tried to ease my pain and fears by controlling her. In doing so, I ruined whatever peace she used to know. I was so hardened. I had become the worst thing that'd ever happened to her. I had become the very thing to her that had first destroyed me.

However, because I was good with words and manipulation, we managed to stay side by side even though the relationship was horrible. By the time she realized what she had gotten herself into, she was in too deep as well and history was repeating itself.

I did not want to be that guy. I did not want to be controlling. I did not want to yell all the time. I did not want to have secrets from everyone, especially the extent to which I was living secretly, abusing alcohol, sex, and money, but it did not feel like I had a choice anymore. It had become a part of me, a part of my character. It was in me.

One moment I would be fine. I would see bits and pieces of my old character that had survived the abuse, abuse I had been put through and put myself through. These little parts of my character were still pleasant; some would even say normal.

The next moment, in the blink of an eye as if someone snapped his fingers, I would become everything my pain and fears had made me—angry, controlling, violent, lashing out like a cornered dog willing to do whatever it takes to get out of the threatening situation. Sometimes it was as simple as realizing for a moment that my girlfriend was running late. Instantly, she became the same threat to me that my old girlfriend had been. I would begin to panic. *Where is she? She is running late for a reason. What could she be doing? I cannot trust her. Who is she with? She is not keeping her word. She is hiding things. I will not let her hurt me! I can't!*

It was as if I were under attack, caught off guard by someone much stronger and bigger than me, and having no chance to survive. It had me by the throat, choking me. It made me want to fight for life, gasp for air, scratch, claw and scream my way out.

It came out of me in many ways, whether it was calling my girlfriend fifty times to make her pick up the phone, or driving around to figure out where she might be and with whom. Usually I would get loud, mean, and harsh to get her to fight with me. I needed to see her fight. I thought, *If she is willing to fight, really fight with me instead of walking away … if I drive her crazy but she does not leave … then I know she cares. Then I'm safe from pain.*

The willingness to do anything to avoid getting hurt drove me to become a man I hated. A second person had been formed inside of me. I felt like I was still just a boy, but this stranger, this man, had grown so strong and was near to overtaking my life. Desiring to live without this man, I considered how I could get rid of him. *Is there only one way out, one way I can get away from all this ... from myself?*

I have to end him.

CHAPTER 6

THE GATES OF HELL

Since we had been together for quite a while, we were accepted into one another's families. We even joined in each other's family getaways. For all I understood back then, I would have claimed I was in love with her.

Business was doing great; it was really going somewhere, especially with all the support I had been receiving from credible industry relationships. Project after project, my name began to become more established, and with that my rates began to climb steadily.

My double life began normalizing, and it became fairly easy for me to manage all the lies required to keep that life a secret. It had become a very large part of who I was. Despite the rocky relationship, the lies, the prostitution, the hard partying, and the heavy drinking, it had in a strange way become a peaceful life for me. A life I knew how to live.

Then one day it hit me; *I want to get married one day.*

That thought presented an invitation for me to start walking down a different road, a road with a different destination. I thought, *If one day I want to get married, I have to at least get the prostitutes out of my life—I will have to quit that. I will have to get myself checked out to make sure I don't carry any disease. If I am clean, I will not have to ever bring up the life that I have lived and I will start heading down this new road, no looking back. A new destination, a new life!*

I never intended to stop sleeping around or to slow down in any other area except the involvement with prostitutes. It just seemed to me that if I got that part straightened out, I could actually make this work. The day I had the thought of marrying her and stopping the meeting with prostitutes would become one of the most powerful turning points in my life.

It just did not turn out the way I planned.

***

After getting myself checked out and coming back clean, I believed I had left the extreme part of my secret life behind. It had been a long time since I had felt like this.

Hope.

The thought of traveling down this new path really did it for me. It was pleasant to feel hope again. For just a moment, life seemed a little more colorful and I imagined what the future would look like. I found myself daring to dream again.

This would become the time when all the strings of bondage that had been placed over me throughout the years began to appear. All the entryways I had given to Satan now started to manifest in power. It felt like it came out of nowhere, without warning.

At the very moment I wanted to turn away from some of the darkness I had committed to, it was as if the gates of hell opened and all of its effort poured out over me. A new season had begun, just like that day in the hotel room. I would find myself many times in places or situations that made me wonder why I was there and how I had gotten there.

The control over my life slipped out of my hands like water. Unannounced, the demands would hit me, the bondage tightening the grip in a way that I could vividly feel. It filled me. A painful fire would fill my chest and burn in a way that made me gasp for air. It was heavy, and it required an amazing amount of effort to carry it around. It took effort to breathe and effort to think clearly; it was disabling.

When it would happen, the only thing my mind could see clearly was the specific thought I was given. It would sit over my mind the same way the fire sat in my chest. It would make me feel so many things at the same time—incredible anxiety, yet ecstasy, powerful energy, yet a heavy weight. The sensation would bring a heightened state of alertness I had never experienced, yet I was only able to think of one thing in those moments: the thought, the instructions lying over my mind.

The fire that filled my chest and the dark thoughts came at random moments. Sometimes, especially when the instructions were things I had never done or desired, I fought them to exhaustion and desperation. It did not take long before I realized it was figuring me out.

That spirit was teaching me. "Any time I fill you, I give you instructions or an assignment. If you obey what I put on your mind and follow through with that assignment, I will lift the fire and the thoughts. If you obey, I will give you peace."

The so-called peace I was granted never lasted long. I tried a number of times to fight that spirit invading my life and the direction it was sucking me into. I did everything and anything I could to help stop my destructive behavior. While I had a moment of clarity and control over my mind I'd burn every bridge I could possibly think of to get away from the extremes of this double life that had formed.

I reasoned through it, trying to guard myself. I tried to approach it strategically; I wrote down ridiculously long passwords for my email addresses and accounts, and after changing them I burned the papers. I blocked off any backup way to get in and recover my contacts. I deleted phone numbers, cut off relationships, and did everything I rationally could to try to get myself out of the demonic assignments and away from the prostitutes. I got another checkup at the hospital and came back clean, determined to be done with the prostitutes, this time for good.

I never was able to leave the prostitutes, not even for a few weeks. I was powerless, being worn out by this spirit and being trained for obedience. It did not take long before it taught me that obedience was unavoidable, and my easiest option was to just get it over with so the spirit would leave me alone for a little while.

Time, after time, after time, it attacked me. As the frequency went up drastically, the darkness got deeper. Soon, men, and all genders ever claimed, became a part of my life in prostitution.

I have never experienced a darkness and a bondage as powerful as I did during that time. It was so strong and deep that it began to alter my very identity. It sought to destroy me to such an extent that I forgot who I used to be. Then, that darkness attempted to shape me into a whole new person, even a whole new gender. Satan had been planning this and working on it in my life for a very long time.

***

As I came into my office one morning, I had a brief thought about God. Strange. The plan for that day had not been to get any work done. I just wanted to watch filth online, but that thought about God bothered me.

I swung my office chair over toward the window and slipped off it onto my knees. There was nothing special that I felt or any presence I was aware of. I did have some kind of a reverence for God in a twisted way, and since I was just done trying to ever be good, I was going to let Him know.

For quite some time, I had tried everything I could to get out. Instead of making progress, it had all gotten so much worse. I was done, ready to stop trying and just give myself over. For some reason, I felt the need to officially put God and this season behind me.

I looked out the window as I said, "God, I cannot change. I don't even think I want to change. If You are real, You have to do it."

I got up. I was done. I sat on my chair and turned on the computer.

***

I finished what I had been typing, and looked out my office window, the same window that I had knelt in front of weeks earlier. Looking back at the computer, I took a drink, a deep breath, and hit the Send button. A confirmation email popped up almost right away saying:

> Your application has been received and is being processed.

Having my application in to become a part-time male prostitute for men, women, and every gender in between made it official. Even though I had been a part of that industry for quite some time, somehow this felt like a tipping point. It almost felt like an accomplishment, as if this was what everything I had been through was leading up to, as if I had been raised up to finally take this position. It felt like I was finally seeing the finish line as if I had an assignment to complete, the very top of the mountain I had been climbing for years now finally within reach. I felt a strange sense of relief.

Satan had been planning this for so long, and his presence was woven throughout some of my oldest memories. I remember how I felt as a little boy when the presence first came. I walked into what felt like a wall of darkness, a presence so thick I could feel and almost taste it. Other times I would wake up at night and the evil presence would be so heavy, I did not dare to move.

One time before falling asleep, I mustered up the courage to run out of my room. Quietly, I hid behind the kitchen door rolled up in a ball. From there, I could hear my parents talking outside on the back porch. Being closer to them made me feel not alone in all the fear that Satan was harassing me with.

Then the back door swung open.

"What are you doing here?" My mom gaped at me, surprised.

"The devil is in my room." I stammered.

"There is nothing there. Go back to your room. Go on. There is nothing wrong."

I felt lonely, abandoned in what felt like a huge battle for me. Never again did I dare to ask for help. I felt ashamed of what I was going through. I felt like it was my fault, like I was creating the problem.

The dreams had also started. I was maybe eight years old.

Night after night I would have the same dream. Alone in a forest, I remember the leaves. Every time, the dream was identical. I saw this small structure. Then I was inside what seemed to be something like a bathroom stall, the kind you would find in school. Something would happen to me in the dream, enter me, and transform me into a girl. It seemed so real.

I woke up sweating, confused, and afraid, full of shame about what I had dreamed, so fearful of it that I never ever wanted to talk about it. The dreams haunted me from night to night, over and over again, always the same.

Eventually, the shame had grown so heavy that the dream started to become a safe place for me. I couldn't possibly share this with anyone. Who would believe or help me? Who would know what to do? I thought, *Here in the dream I do not have to hide. I don't have to be on guard. I don't have to keep a secret. Here, I can be myself.*

Now, over a decade later, it was finally happening. I read the confirmation email again.

Yes, relief. Now I can finally start living as myself.

CHAPTER 7

THE ARMORY

"Yeah, I have many unregistered firearms. There is no registration process needed, since they are regarded as collectibles. I've been collecting them for years and have never had a problem."

I zoned out. I had just overheard a conversation that caught me off guard and was trying to process the information. I thought of the possibilities and the control I could gain, especially since my list of enemies was growing. I had made some serious threats in the past, but if this was true, it would change everything. The thoughts were reassuring, comforting a deep place inside of me.

As soon as I was alone, I got on the computer to verify; I could not believe it. If I was willing to put up the money, it was possible. Confused but pleasantly overwhelmed, I realized that this unlocked a whole new set of options for me. All I needed to do was find new-condition firearms preceding a precise production date. I would avoid registration, a paper trail, and all questions.

***

After finding that hole in the law, I began scouring the net, purposing to find myself 9-millimeter and .22 caliber weapons that could handle modern ammunition. It is nearly impossible to quickly become a firearm owner in the Netherlands, but this temporary hole in the law was my way around it. It would allow me to purchase firearms without doing any paperwork or registration.

Now, it was going to cost me a pretty penny and some legwork. First, I had to find the right unused or lightly used revolver models up for sale or auction then find someone willing to take the cash with no questions asked.

After some time and a lot of research, I finally had the first pickup arranged. The instructions were:

> Park at the apartment building at two a.m., text
> me, and I'll give you a code to enter the complex.
> Don't wear a coat or baggy pants, I will have eyes
> on you.

It was raining. I had gotten there early and was waiting anxiously in the dark parking lot. At two a.m. I sent the text:

> I'm here.

I received the door code as I was walking up to the scarcely lit entryway. I punched in the numbers while looking around, wondering if they were watching me, and from where.

I got in the elevator and hit the button for the correct floor. Adrenaline rushed through my body, heightening my senses. When I reached the floor, it was almost as if the elevator doors opened in slow motion. With the cash burning in my pocket and my heart racing, I stepped into the hallway and sent another text as instructed. A door quickly opened behind me down the hall. I had been given the wrong apartment number to catch me off guard, allowing some element of surprise.

As I got sized up, I was motioned to come into the apartment. I say apartment, but it seemed more like an armory. I had never seen anything like it. Once the man was convinced I was not carrying, his next sentence hit me unexpectedly and hard as if it woke me up.

He asked, "Do you have the cash?"

I pulled the cash out of my pocket and handed it over. He briefly nodded and motioned toward a box on the table. "It's all there."

Then it really hit me; the number of thoughts that flooded my mind were countless. This meeting was almost over before I realized it had started. My mind now worked at lightning speed while I glanced at the wall covered with weapons.

I had to make my next decision. As I picked up and checked the box, I thought ahead and realized there was no way around it; I had completely missed it. The hardest part of this whole meeting was not in setting it up or finding the contacts. It was still to come.

After all this effort, coming up with the money, following all instructions, showing up alone, ignoring all danger, and keeping this meeting a secret from everyone ... now, here all alone in this room at two a.m., I had to face the hardest part.

I was going to have to turn my back on this guy to walk out of the room, leaving myself completely exposed. *If I will ever get shot in the back, it will be here.*

I had to make the most vulnerable move in the most dangerous situation, leaving myself at the mercy of a stranger. This was the last place on earth where that felt like a reasonable option.

Alternatives flashed through my mind for a split second as I weighed my chances and considered the possible outcomes. As far as I could see, trying to shoot my way out of this would not end up favorably for me.

I took a deep breath. Then I turned. It felt like everything was happening in slow motion. The anticipation of what might happen next grew with each step I took toward the door. It seemed like the lock clicked so loudly as it was secured behind me. *I made it. Now I'll have even more control.*

***

As my anger grew, so did my desire to destroy people who offended me or got in the way of my desires. Planning to use my newly acquired weapons, not only for the purpose of enforcing my will but to manifest my hatred toward people who offended me, gave me a sense of power and strange peace. It felt like the lives of anyone who angered me rested in my hands.

A while back, I had publicly humiliated a guy. I didn't even know his name but found out where he lived and his schedule. Ever since I took his girl, he had been running his mouth.

It's the third time he has attacked my reputation. I have warned him and considered my options, but I'm left with no other choice. I'll have to take his life. I gave him a fair chance.

For a few days, I had been planning it—how and where to do it—but most importantly where to get rid of the body. I made sure I had the transporting of the body figured out and asked myself where I would choose to dump it. After coming up with every "good" place I could think of and writing them down, I picked a very contradicting kind of spot compared to what the list was reflecting.

I have to do this in a way that would make it appear that I could have never done it. Making sure the body is never found is the hardest and most important part. If I figure out in detail how my logic would go about every step of getting rid of the body and then I do the opposite, when they come looking through my life, if

I am ever suspected, there would be nothing in my life or psyche that would point in the hidden direction.

***

I had gotten used to the process. Now, here alone with the office blinds closed, I leaned over and opened the drawers to look at them. I had more by now, they occupied the right side of my desk. The left side had my company administration; it gave me a strong feeling of power and authority, that I was somewhat in control while making enemies.

I knew my office well. Being a perfectionist helped me run my company in design, but it also made me notice all the little things. One morning when I came into the office, some of those little things were different.

For weeks, I had not been able to shake the feeling that someone had been in my office, and I sat down to think it over once again. *I know someone has been here, even though I never forget to lock up. Who is it and why? Does it have something to do with the guns?*

As I sat there trying to figure out if I was crazy or onto something, the memories of conversations I'd had came to me so clearly, all the dots now connecting in my head. Picking a lock, weapons, my office location … there was only one man that in covert ways had mentioned or asked me about all the above in the last months.

I knew what had happened. I could never prove it, nor would I confront him. I figured my best move was to have him think that I was in the dark about it. If he did not know that I was onto him, maybe that gave me an advantage.

My phone vibrated at the edge of my desk. It wasn't my girlfriend's name on the screen; it was another woman. I read the message and checked my watch. *I have to go if I want to make it on time for this overnight party trip with the other woman.*

By the time I locked the office door behind me, I had a solid alibi in place to tell my girlfriend and family for this unplanned night away. As usual, they wouldn't suspect a thing.

***

The next morning, I walked down the street with the sun on my face trying to ignore the pounding headache souvenir I carried around from the previous night. I made my way to the nearest grocery store; The woman I had partied with had explained to me how to get there, as I wanted to buy us some breakfast.

As I walked out of the store carrying two full bags, I saw the parked Mercedes. A shiver went down my spine, and my heart started racing. I felt like I knew this car as the one belonging to the man I believed had secretly gone through my office. I tried to maintain my pace and composure as I pieced it all together in my head.

Did he take me on as a PI job? He sought for more than just something in my office? Why is he here? Why follow me here? Where is my car?

With a sigh of relief, I remembered that I had parked far away, realizing the chance would be very small that he would find my car and go through that as well.

Why exactly is he here?

Considering that he may have had eyes on me as I realized all this, I tried to look for him without being obvious, but I never caught a glimpse of him. *Could I have it all wrong?* I decided to let it go, and I returned to the apartment with the groceries.

CHAPTER 8

NOVEMBER 4

A few weeks later, I was driving home after another wild party night. I was almost there. As I drove into town, I caught myself again. *What in the world is wrong with me?*

As soon as I realized it, I stopped myself. It had been happening more often lately. Randomly, I would find myself whistling or humming songs about Jesus that I had learned growing up. Driving home from partying or prostitution, the words would come into my mind so clearly that I started singing. I felt so embarrassed every time I realized what was happening, I quickly put a stop to it. *What is happening? I have not sung these songs in a decade. What in the world is wrong with me?*

***

Friday, November 4, God and I had opposing plans; I did not have the slightest idea what He was up to.

I was in my office when the phone rang. *Strange. He must have come back early from his business trip.* I hit the Answer button. My girlfriend's father invited me to come over to their house. I felt something nice when we hung up. It always had me excited when I was involved in family activities, especially when others took the initiative to make sure I could be there. It made me feel like I was wanted and loved. What I didn't know was that the private eye I had discovered following me and going through my office had been collecting information for him.

I quickly finished up cleaning my piece and stashed it separately from the ammo. I hurried out of the office and got on the road. Once I arrived at the house and walked in, I made my way toward the living room.

Before I reached it, my girlfriend's father motioned as he passed me and quietly said, "We are sitting in the kitchen."

As I turned around, I caught a glimpse of discomfort on his face. *Was it the travel? Back pain? Business? Or something else …*

By the time I sat down, my girlfriend had joined as well. As her mother looked at me from where she sat at the table, her expression seemed blank.

Excited to spend time with the family, and assuming we would share some good food, I leaned in from my comfortable chair and asked, "How was your trip?"

Without looking up at me, he replied, "It was okay."

After what I felt was pleasant small talk, the conversation abruptly began to take a turn.

He asked, "Is there something you have to share with us?"

I made an ignorant face. "No, not really."

Quickly, I gave my girlfriend a look to try to read anything off her, but she did not give me much. *Okay, I am just going to have to play it cool, make them show their cards first.*

As the awkward silence continued and pressure built, her mom blurted out, "Don't you have something to say about your dishonesty? Isn't there someone you want to tell us about?"

Instantly, my girlfriend's face changed. I read the unbelief and panic there as she became overwhelmed with emotion and spoke up.

"Mom, what are you talking about? What is she talking about?"

I replied, "I don't know."

Her mom continued, "What do you mean, you don't know?"

All the gates inside of me locked in place. I calculated. I needed to take control of this situation before it actually became a threat to me. My anger was building as accusations came my way. I was not giving them anything and they felt it.

"You are not honest with us." My girlfriend's dad continued. "You're not faithful to our daughter. We want you to tell her the truth, and I am making the decision for her. She will no longer be your girlfriend."

This is it; I am done. Who in the ******* world do these guys think they ******* are? No one speaks to me that way, no one!

I pushed back. "I'm not going to have this conversation. I am not going to talk with you guys. I will talk to her alone in her room."

"We have received the evidence from our source, and it is sitting on our lawyer's desk." Her dad responded. "Know that I instructed him to publish all findings if anything were to happen to us tonight."

The break-in … the following me around … it was not just about the weapons at all. They hired him?

Her father got up and as a painful but powerful gesture of love, he stood behind me and put his hand firmly on my shoulder, just a split second longer than usual. He shook me a little, then I felt his hand leave. I was so full of anger that I did not accept his gesture. I could not receive it. I pushed it out of my mind and took her to her bedroom.

Back in control, I looked at her and tried to downplay it all. I told her, "I just made a mistake and kissed another girl."

Leaving her behind, distraught, I made my way out of the house as I heard her parents ensure the breakup in an effort to protect her. I closed that front door behind me for the last time.

Every physical step I took walking away from the house, I thought about the course of action I had to take. By the time I got off the property, I was ready to deal with this. I took in a deep breath while I stared at my car. Then, I moved on toward revenge.

Someone has talked; someone is going to pay for this. Someone sided against me, I cannot let that slide.

As I got in my car, I organized my thoughts and took my phone out of my pocket. While scrolling through my phone, I saw a name. He was actually the first person I had

thought of. I would not have called him a friend, maybe more
of a strategic partner for when I had to deal with any kind of
troublesome people. We had first talked about it a while ago
when I was looking for some muscle and asked him to help
me set that up. I wanted to have some guys available to send a
physical message whenever I had a situation that called for it.

I skipped his number for now and dialed the number of
my best friend. I told him, "I need you to come and meet me
at the waterfront. We broke up. It is over, but I need your
help to figure out what happened and what we are going to
do about it. Meet me ASAP."

I parked at the waterfront and tried to piece it all together
while I waited for him.

I saw headlights ... *It must be him.*

He parked next to me and started making his way over to
my car as he asked through the open window, "What in the
world is going on? You guys broke up?" He sat down in the
passenger seat, confused.

Even though it was clear to him from the party life alone
that I was no trustworthy boyfriend, he had no idea to what
extent I was living a double life. As I filled him in, he seemed
genuinely surprised at everything that was happening.

I explained, "Listen, her parents made her break up with me. Someone has talked about me and another girl. We need to figure out where this is coming from and deal with it."

We sat together in the car, and phone call after phone call provided dead ends until we finally caught a clear lead. Knowing now what direction to take, we needed to come up with a plan. After discussing a few different options, we decided to put it to rest until the next day, not knowing that I would never be the same person again after that night.

As he drove off, I was already thinking about my next challenge—going home. I gave my dad a quick call to see if he was home. I told him I had to talk to him about something. I could tell from his tone that he knew it was something serious. He said it would be a few minutes, but that he would be on his way home soon.

My mind worked overtime trying to prepare for a meeting I could not avoid.

A half hour later, I took a deep breath as I pulled up to the house. *I got this.*

CHAPTER 9

THE BREATH

My mom was shopping in London, England, at the time. I got out of my car and walked toward the front door, grateful I only had to deal with my dad that evening. I walked through the front door, still deciding on my opening sentence. My dad met me in the hallway ... *Out of time.*

I simply blurted out, "We broke up."

Dad asked, "What do you mean? No way, what happened?"

I replied, "Yeah, stupid. I kissed another girl."

He turned toward me. "She would never break up with you for that."

We walked into the living room. My dad sat down in the chair across the room, and I took the couch. At this point, I was willing to go as far as to admit that I had cheated. That was a small calculated loss, small enough for me and big enough for them to believe that that was it. I was confident that if I sold it well, they would never even think about digging any deeper.

In this situation, copping to alleged cheating was almost ironic. Considering the lifestyle I was protecting, this move was a five-star step in damage control. If I made it look good for a few weeks, it would blow over. That was the plan.

"So," Dad pressed further. "Tell me what happened?"

With my eyes to the side and making sure no emotions crossed my face, I took a deep breath. Everything seemed to slow down. It honestly felt like I lived a lifetime during that one breath. I thought about how to word the lie that I was about to weave into the tapestry of my life. It needed to fit in with all the other lies and fortify the protection around my deepest secrets. I would give a little and keep all the rest.

I laid my eyes back on my father. I had regained my composure, and I was confident that I had control over the outcome of this night. I was about to start using that breath to set my plan in motion. Then, before I got a chance, in that one breath, it happened… For the first time in my life, God spoke to me.

If you come back now, we are going to do it together and we are going to go all the way. If you do not come back now, you will never come back.

All my life, I had heard things about God but never that He would speak, really speak, to people like me. His presence was so loving and thick, yet His holiness began burning. I could feel it with all my being.

Instantly, I knew He was the God of Light and Truth. I knew He was inviting me, that He would be forever with me if I would take hold of His invitation.

He showed me His heart and in a split second, He filled me with understanding. This was not about me getting a prayer life or reading the Bible. He did not care about making me a good church person. This was about my life. God was trying to save my life!

There was nothing He wanted from me. He just wanted me! Nothing was clearer; God the Light, God the Truth was speaking to me. He showed me that coming to Him, and being with Him from here on out, required me to come into the truth and into the light.

God gave me clear understanding of what He meant the moment He said it.

If you come back now …

Coming back to my creator meant that every secret and every deed that was hidden in darkness and kept safe in shadows had to come completely into the Light. No longer could I trust in lies and leave the truth unspoken. I had to come into the Truth, all of me.

It was clear that if I, with all I really was, would be visible in the Light, my family would distance themselves from me. I could see that it would ruin my company. There would be no more hope of getting back with my girlfriend, and there would be a total loss of whatever image I had. At the time, it meant losing everything, but I would have Him.

There was a clear choice. I did have the option to get away with claiming only to have cheated on my girlfriend, and that was something I could see myself recover from quickly. It would be a small price to pay for the life I was hiding, but it was His thick, loving yet Holy presence and the way He spoke to me that made it hardly a choice at all. He would be with me forever.

We are going to do it together, and we are going to go all the way.

All the things that I have done or that have been done to me, all the things I have hidden and buried, a decade of garbage and

*unspeakable secrets, too much work, too much pain, too much …
but He will be with me.*

He did not ask me to do this alone. He did not require
me to fix it or clean it up. It would no longer be my mess. He
wanted all of me—my past, present and future. He wanted me
to be His burden. He asked me to lay it all down, to entrust
Him, the Light and the Truth, with myself.

If you don't come back now, you will never come back.

The Lord was not recruiting. He was not looking for a
hard worker. He was looking to save someone who was lost,
broken, and on his way to hell.

He spoke to me with a bleeding heart. He spoke to me,
crying out as if He were losing the love of His life!

That one breath came out of me as a heavy sigh from
an old heart. In that one breath, everything was different. I
looked at my father, who had no idea that in one breath my
whole world had changed. I instantly understood, *God loves
me.*

I blurted out, "I slept with another girl."

Speaking that truth, uncovering the darkness, was like I
moved closer toward the Lord of my soul one more step.

I continued. "I slept with many girls."

My dad's face changed. I saw unbelief, maybe pain, yet he seemed calm. The presence of God was growing; by now I had started weeping. I wanted to let it all out. *I want to run to my Lord, to the Light and Truth, but I cannot. I cannot share these things.* My flesh and Satan were locking arms to fight for ground. The thoughts flooded in …

Don't share more. I can't say these things. I cannot transform the darkness that I am a part of into words. This darkness is too heavy; it is not made to be put into words. The words will be too heavy; they will kill my world, everything I love.

Then, there was clarity.

No! God did not say I had to do this alone, I will take it to Him.

I cried out silently, *Lord, I can't speak these things, but burn me clean.*

Time and time again, the Lord's presence would fall heavier as I prayed that little prayer, and every time, His presence came so thick. The way He was with me provided the way forward.

I continued. "I've been with many prostitutes."

My father remained calm as I felt things violently changing all over me. I could almost audibly hear shackles bursting apart under the pressure and power of Truth. Healing started to flow more and more into all my wounds as I took refuge in the Light. The Lord burned so hot but so lovingly. There was such an urgency in Him and in His presence. I could feel the truth welling up inside of me ready to burst out, as if the truth was being demanded to come forth in His presence.

Again, I prayed, *Lord, I can't speak these things, but burn me clean.*

The Lord would come closer, and I would let go, one step at a time. As I handed over my life to Him and entrusted Him with all I was and all I ever would be, He made me more and more truthful inside and out, step by step.

"I've been with men. I've been with transsexuals."

One step at a time, He led me into the Truth and Light. He led me to Himself by faith, trust, and repentance, and He truly held my hand and carried my weight with His presence. With every feeble step I made, His power just showed up. Never did He let me do it alone, ever since I trusted Him just a tiny little bit. He has never let the weight of sin fall on me again.

On that couch I was changed, forgiven, made brand new, and lighter. It was as if I had carried a heavy backpack for years, and for the first time, I was learning to walk without it. I felt light as a feather.

I could not stop weeping; I could feel again, finally feel again! The big black empty hole was gone! I felt so whole. Never again did I feel the kind of loneliness and powers that had moved me into bad decisions so many times. My drive for career, achievements, and the need to live up this life and make something of it, all gone!

I was free—at peace.

If you ever have the privilege of speaking with my dad, ask him and he will tell you like he told me, "I still can't explain it, but something came over me when Stan started to tell the truth, and all I could do and all I felt was love."

***

For the next few months of healing, from the moment I woke up until I went to bed at night, I would weep almost constantly. The Lord's presence was so heavy. When I opened my eyes in the morning, He was waiting for me. With tears, I greeted Him, and tears were my final prayer at night. Constantly, He was healing me, cleaning me up, and feeding me. With my tears, brokenness and pain flowed out of me into His hands as He held me. His presence was the healing balm of restoration constantly surrounding me.

Jesus Christ saved me!

CHAPTER 10

THE HOLY SPIRIT

The first Saturday of my new life, all hate and anger were gone, no longer fueling my self-centered way of thinking and living. Finally free from the desire to always get justice or revenge, I now just wanted to tell the truth.

I drove back home to speak to my mom, as she had flown back from shopping in England. As I turned off my car, I realized I did not feel heavy or any shame. Nothing told me to not speak again all those things I had done in my life. All I felt was peace, which was not what I had expected. I thought it would be heavy and challenging every time I spoke about my past.

My mom did not really know anything yet. My dad had mentioned that I needed to talk with her. In all reality,

I expected to have at least a measure of the fight I had
experienced the first time I had brought it all into the light.
Instead, I felt more excited than anything, excited to let my
mom know what Jesus had done in spite of me.

Ready, I opened the front door and walked into the house.
I saw my mom at the end of the hallway by the kitchen. She
turned to me. The moment she rested her eyes on mine, her
face went into shock.

Her hand flew up in front of her mouth as she gasped for
air, then shouted, "Your eyes are different!"

Not really knowing how to respond, I just hugged her.
We went to sit down in the kitchen, and I started sharing with
my mom like I had done with my father. It was so easy to just
share and talk about my past and failures now that the Lord
had spoken to me. On top of that, the incredible truth that
someone like me could be forgiven and set free in a moment
through Jesus Christ just made it so much more attractive to
share it all.

It was hard for my mom. With eyes full of unbelief and
worry, she looked away while I spoke. At first, it was extremely
hard for my mom to accept the fact that her son had ended up
so deep, in need of total saving. She found it hard to accept

that she was not to blame for the path I had gone down. In the end she blurted out, "I've asked Jesus many times to save you, but if I had known it would happen like this, I don't think I would have ever asked."

The reason that I could only feel love for my mom in that moment and no pain at all, was because I was not alone there. The Lord was there. He had filled me with divine purpose and surrounded me with His presence.

Not really knowing what to do with me, my parents asked me to talk to our pastor, and I gladly agreed to meet with him.

***

The following Monday, I went to my office, sat down at my desk, turned on the computer, and planned to look for a sermon. Then a desire hit me. It was faint but I knew this feeling; it came up suddenly. It definitely did not have power compared to what I used to experience before, but it scared me, nonetheless.

Even though the demonic authority had been broken over my life, I was intimidated by this desire rising from my own flesh. The desire was so clear; I wanted attention, more than just from the Lord. I wanted a girl to reach out to me, to text me, even if it meant for me to reach out first to then see someone respond to me. It was faint but clear.

Instantly I fell to my knees and said, "Jesus I'm feeling this, but I don't ever want that again. I do not want to text anyone."

Just like that, it was as if the Lord picked something off me again. When I got up, the desire was gone, just gone.

***

That same week, as I was talking to the Lord alone in my office, He came into the room. I loved the sweet time we spent together. To finally belong and always be wanted was so soothing. It was as if He got behind me and placed a ginormous injection needle in my back and emptied it out in one quick go. He filled me.

Caught off guard, I gasped for air. Understanding, faith, divine clarity, and power filled me up beyond what I could contain. Instantly, in a way I had never experienced before, I had two clear thoughts.

I already have enough faith to be saved, so this couldn't be for me.

If this is for me, I might need this to get through persecution, or this is for others and I'm called to work for Him my entire life.

Again, everything was different. Even though the Lord had been so intimate and close since the previous Friday, now it felt like I had gone from black-and-white to full-color HD-TV with surround sound. Wondering what all this meant and would mean in the future, I just sat in His presence.

I had never heard about the baptism with the Holy Spirit being given to people. All I knew at that point was whatever the Lord had shown and taught me so far. Later I would hear stories from believers and recognize the same things in my own life with the Lord. As I first read the Bible, I would see all the stories and get to know the promises the Lord has made. As I was learning, I realized that I had experienced these things with the Lord already. God was keeping these promises to me even before I knew about them! I was stunned, shocked that God would keep His promises the way you see Him do it in the Bible, even to someone like me!

He kept confirming to me time after time that He was the God of the Bible. He would fulfill a promise in me, and then I would usually read about it within the next twenty-four hours. He would show me on the page word for word what I had just been through with Him, or I would read something that the Holy Spirit had just taught me in prayer. There was nothing in the life that Jesus was giving me that He left me to figure out on my own; He always did it together with me.

***

On my way to our pastor's house, I was filled with excitement to tell him about the things Jesus had done in my life and to my sin. I was fascinated with the doorbell as I walked up to the front door. It was awesome and old fashioned. You had to grab the knob and pull it straight out; it was connected to all kinds of levers that made a cast bell swing on the inside of the house.

Someone I didn't recognize came to the door. She welcomed me into the home and asked me to wait in the office. After a few moments, the pastor came in and sat down as he asked what this was about and how I was doing.

"I'm saved! I got to know Jesus!" I blurted out in excitement.

As I started to share my whole past and how Jesus had forgiven me and set me free, I quickly began to recognize confusion on his face. The confusion I suspected he felt was confirmed by the way he asked questions.

He was not convinced that Jesus and I knew each other, and that Jesus had done for me what I was testifying about. This was unexpected, but it did not hurt. The Stan I knew would raise his voice and use words to wound and attack in this situation, but everything had changed. As a matter of fact, all I could feel was love and a growing desire for the pastor to see what I had seen. If I could only just somehow show him …

The Holy Spirit was so close and gave me love and grace for people. I had never experienced that before! It surprised me; He had changed all kinds of things about me and in me already. In many ways I could not recognize myself in the way I responded to people. Not just on the outside but even in my feelings and emotions. I was changed!

As we ended the conversation, the pastor said he doubted that I was telling the truth. He asked if we could talk again but with another person there.

I replied, "Absolutely, gladly. Thank you."

The following talk with the pastor and an elder from the church was more disappointing. The questions proved that there was more doubt in their minds about what I was testifying about than joy or gladness. Most people did not recognize that God was moving. I so wanted them to see, and I was doing my best to describe the experiences and events I had been through with this loving and righteous God, that He came to me to pursue and save me, a true sinner. But I just seemed to be hitting walls.

People increasingly thought I was making it all up. Eventually, their minds were set and they told me they wanted me to see a Christian-based psychiatrist. So aware of the nearness of the Holy Spirit and without feeling or thinking something negative toward anyone, I simply told them, "I'm more than willing to do whatever you would like me to do. I have nothing to hide anymore. I am free."

***

Eventually, after a few sessions of filling out questionnaires and testifying about my past, my guilt, and the hurts Jesus had freed me from and forgiven me for, the pastor asked me to meet with him again to talk about my progress with the psychiatrist.

"How do you think it has been going so far at the counseling office?" he asked.

I answered, "Very well."

Inside I was so hopeful, excited to possibly see joy and celebration in his eyes, a twinkling that decorates the eyes of someone who can see that it is finished.

Then the pastor said, "According to the report from the doctor, it didn't go so well. I called him. He was somewhat frustrated, because everything that he heard from you points toward the fact that you don't believe you have a problem anymore. I don't think we can help you."

Why did they not see? While I was living my horrible past life with a thousand secrets, no one was worried. Now that I had told everyone the truth, everyone was worried! No one seemed to really know what to do with me anymore. *How come they do not recognize that a sinner got saved?*

Wondering why all of this was happening, I slowly walked back home. I knew how my old self would have responded in such situations. I just kept thanking the Lord for changing me already so deeply. It was so surprising to see myself handle these situations and people so differently.

It took a long, long time before I began to get used to my new self, saved by Jesus Christ. All the changes He made kept catching me off guard. Seeing my life being affected by the Spirit of Christ showed me that He cared so much more about every part of my life than I could have ever imagined!

He was teaching me one step and one event at a time that He cares and takes responsibility for every part of my life. To learn deep in my spirit that I would never again face anything alone began building an unbreakable peace.

CHAPTER 11

A DESIRE TO SHARE

I got to my office that morning with the intention of diving back into getting to know the Bible; but as I was praying, the presence of the Lord came, and the Holy Spirit showed me a vision for the very first time. There was no sound, but I could see myself before I got saved, stuck in my old life. Somehow, I could sense all the sin that I had continually chosen. All my old, hidden darkness was there.

In the vision, I saw myself standing in what looked like thick mud. Even though the mud only reached halfway up my chest, it had covered me from head to toe as if I had been baptized in it. I was willfully living and engaging in all that unspeakable filth. It looked like I had merged with the darkness, like I was a part of it.

Then the vision changed. I took my eyes off the old me down there in the mud to look up. Then, I saw the Lord. He was looking down on the mud-covered Stan. He had been watching me all that time. But despite everything I did, and all that was done to me, He never looked away in disgust! He never looked away!

Instead, I saw such a loving look in His eyes while He looked down on me stuck in my sin and secret life. Seeing that love in His eyes changed something in me once again. Before I had gotten saved, before I ever cared about Him or ever felt regret or conviction, He loved me.

Right there while I had the vision, I could not see the Lord in defined shape or really see His face, but somehow the vision revealed clearly the way He looked at me. He was just waiting for me down there all that time to look up so I could finally see that look in His eyes. *He desires me. He loves me. He waits for me.*

The way God looks at you will change you!

The realization that the cross of Jesus Christ had the power to nullify my sins, change me continually and reveal that the Father's eyes have been filled with love and care for me all along, gave birth to a thought. *This is the way the Father looks at people despite their sins and choices?*

All I could think of were the people who did not know, like the Stan in that vision stuck and covered in filth but not looking up ever. *They don't know… I didn't know.* I thought I had to change myself and my actions. I thought I had to become somewhat good, or at least better.

I thought I had to fight my way out. I was looking for a way out of my mud. Working to get out of it made me feel that God would see all that work and it would convince Him that I was sorry. Instead, all I was proving was that the clay I was stuck in had power to quickly suck me down deeper with every move I made. I was looking for ways to possibly get some of the dirt off me to make myself more presentable. I did not know that it was already finished! All I kept proving was that I couldn't do any of it.

***

It was a new morning at my office, this one full of new convictions. The Holy Spirit was giving me clear instructions on what to do with a whole bunch of stuff I had accumulated before I knew Christ that needed to disappear out of my life. I got busy gathering the items.

As I tied up the garbage bag, the Lord showed me that He wanted me to throw this out at a specific gas station. Although a little confused by the odd instructions, I decided to listen to Him. As I got into my car, the Lord told me to drive a completely different route than what I intended to. It was so specific, even I thought it was a little far-fetched.

Just about halfway there, I was driving on a two-way, single-lane highway when I saw a car stopped at a crossroad on the opposite side of the highway. I thought the driver had seen me. As I drove by the car, he pulled out and quickly tried to turn on to the highway in front of me at the very moment I was passing him. I hit the brakes and swerved. I don't know how we didn't collide. We both pulled over to the right side of the road.

As I grabbed my door latch, the Lord spoke clearly. *Ask this man if he knows Me.*

The presence of the Lord rushed upon me, and quickly I rushed out of the car. I saw an older man walking my way, and his face spoke clearly. He felt horrible about what could have been a significant accident and seemed pretty shaken up.

I blurted out, "We barely made it out of that one without a ding, didn't we?" I stretched out my hand. As he shook it, I asked, "Do you know the Lord Jesus Christ?"

The man replied, "No!"

He almost seemed to answer out of reflex as if he had just recognized me as a threat.

I responded, "Sir, if you know Jesus you are ready to face death at any time. I have my Bible in my car. Let me get it. I want to give it to you."

As I turned around and grabbed the Bible, he said, "No, no, no. I can't take that. I have my own Bible. I'm a Jehovah's Witness."

I said again, "Well, don't forget sir, if you know Jesus, you are ready to face death at any time."

As I got into the car, I rejoiced with all my heart. I understood it may not have looked like a success at first glance, but I knew who sent me out there. I know the Holy Spirit had planted a seed in that man's heart that he would not easily get rid of.

I was learning that My Lord wants people to know what He has done for them, and that absolutely anyone can experientially, personally know Him. He wants to know you and be known by you.

What blew me away and still gets me excited to this day was that my Lord was willing to use someone with a past like mine, someone who used to build Satan's kingdom and destroy people's lives. God turns it all around and then uses that person to bring life and hope. When the Lord uses me as a vessel in any way, I cannot help but feel like the Lord is rubbing it in Satan's face. It's like He is saying to Satan, "Your power and dominion are broken! You lose."

My Jesus chose to present Himself as weak as possible on the cross, yet He still couldn't help but obliterate all the power and dominion of Satan in a way that shook the world.

CHAPTER 12

SWITCHING CAREERS

It had been two weeks since Jesus saved me. How I knew from the very start I cannot explain, but I had such clear understanding that the God I had met was the God of the Bible. Doubt never got to me, so as soon as I had the opportunity, I picked up an old Bible and started reading. First, I mainly read in the New Testament then increasingly more of the Old.

I wept through almost every page, because it felt like it was all written for me and about me, about my situations, about the things I had been through and felt inside. Everything I felt now that God had come into my life and the things He was doing in me, I would literally see described in words when I opened that Bible. God had this all written down and explained in words so that now I could begin to understand and share what had happened to, and in, me. I cried out many times while reading, "This is about me! It is about me!"

Overwhelmed, I realized that God knew me so deeply, and that He understood! God wanted me to know that He understands me, that He is interested and involved in every part of me. All of it made me feel so at home, so wanted. I felt like I finally, truly belonged.

The more I shared the unlimited hope and potential in Christ for anyone, especially if they are a sinner, the more I became aware that I cared for people. I felt love, a painful love, for all those people who did not and do not know that it's over already, that God is done dealing with the problem of sin we caused. The more time I spent with my Lord, the more I wanted people to see what I had seen, to know Him, and to be at peace.

***

I settled into my office, and after reading some chapters in the Bible, I longed to talk to Jesus. As I knelt on my office floor, time seemed to disappear. His nearness was so real. His voice washed over me with healing and comfort.

When I got up, I found the website of my favorite ministry and started listening to their online service. I wept a lot, but today I felt something new. *I want to be like them. I want to help and contribute. Where is it? How do I reach them?* I found the contact page on the website and began typing. I wrote an email to this ministry whose services and events I had been listening to since I had gotten saved. In the email, I described my past and how the Lord had saved me and changed so many things in me overnight. I wrote of the things that I had fought to change for years yet only made them worse, but Jesus had done the impossible for a sinner like me. He had changed me, and that was, humanly speaking, just impossible. I wrote to them about how compelled I felt to share with others about Jesus Christ.

On the bottom of the contact page, I read that a typical response would take three business days. Thinking that they would be all over this, I began waiting. I believed they would realize God had done something great and that He was with me. I expected a welcome and open response. I expected to hear back from them quickly.

Day after day, I checked my email, and after day three I began to get anxious. *But it could be so many things, so many reasons. I will wait.* After two weeks of waiting impatiently, I sent a second email. I addressed it to the head of the ministry and urged him:

> It is just me and the Lord every day. I am willing to do anything. If you would just let me carry chairs to help set up the events, anything. I just want to be around people who love Him and are as excited about Him as I am. I want to be around people who know Him.

I was close to desperate to get a response and to be a part of that ministry, to be a part of the seemingly successful way others were reaching people for Christ together. I longed to see the desires that were being birthed inside of me come to pass. It must have been one obedient and praying team, because I still have not received an email back. The Lord was setting up other things and beginning to put things in motion I could not see.

Having a hard time seeing my need for "walking through" God's process, I became almost obsessive with finding the way that would lead to what God had shown me in my heart. I was convinced that if I got the way right, then I would see myself arrive in the purpose He had given to me. I was willing to do almost anything to make sure I didn't miss that way.

The Lord, however, was going to teach me not to look for the way things could come to pass, but instead to look to the One who gave the desire and would bring it to pass by His power and miraculous ways.

***

It was December, almost two months since Jesus and I had started to get to know each other. Once saved, I began the journey of discovering who God is. He already fully knew me, but it didn't feel like that. The discovery process I was going through didn't feel out of balance. He never made me feel like I was behind, the way that you can feel when you fall behind in school and you receive special attention because you were not strong or smart enough to do as well as others.

It would have been so reasonable for me to feel that way in His presence and among His people because I had gotten saved as an adult, but it never felt that way. He also never made me feel like it was just me getting to know Him, and that He already knew everything about me. He knew all things, don't get me wrong, and it easily could have felt that way. Yet instead, I felt like He wanted to get to know me. He revealed day after day in so many ways that He is interested in me, intrigued even. *He feels privileged to spend time with me; that is how my Lord makes me feel every day.*

***

Still waiting and hoping for a response to my email, I felt slightly confused that it was taking so long, over six weeks by now. I was not used to something not working out when it had to do with Jesus and being saved. I was used to the impossible always working out when Jesus was involved, but this whole ministry thing made me feel stuck. However, God was about to make a change when I least expected it.

A group of my friends was going to get together for an evening out at a local restaurant and bowling center. Eager to always seize an opportunity to talk about my Lord to my friends, I made sure I would be there.

That evening, one of my buddies brought a friend of his who I did not really know, so he was in my crosshairs from the moment we shook hands. We made small talk and as soon as I could, I brought up the Lord and started sharing about my

Jesus and how anyone can get to know Him, and be forgiven and made new.

"Yeah, I know him," he said.

I thought, *Guilty until proven innocent.*

So, I kept up with the conversation, eager to see and find out if he and Jesus really knew each other, if he would know things that only Jesus reveals. I needed to know that he was saved to make sure I did not need to worry about his soul. What I did not know was that the Lord set up this meeting for me, to make a change in my life. God wasn't seeking to use me that night. He was setting me up to receive.

Toward the end of the conversation, the guy told me, "You know, you're so in love with Jesus. I volunteer at this ministry, and they use all kinds of sports, mainly soccer, to reach youth in big cities. A lot of the families they serve are poor and they are really making a difference in the lives of these kids. They serve and spread the gospel message. They are starting a big event tomorrow in Rotterdam. You normally must sign up and get approved as a worker a few weeks in advance, but why don't you give them a call? They would love to have you."

As he was talking, in my own pride I disregarded most of what he said. I thought to myself, *Jesus does not need another person to speak into my life. You may not realize this, but He speaks to me. I do not even like soccer.*

Growing up, soccer was by far the most popular sport. I played but was always one of the last ones who got picked when the captains chose their teams. It had worn a wound into my self-esteem to where I began to avoid the game. I had decided to not like the game anymore. That way, I didn't have to deal with the way it felt when I was waiting for my name to be called, not because I was eager to play but because I hoped to avoid the pain of being last pick. The last picks are not chosen for what they bring to the team and instead are chosen based on who will do the least damage to the team and its chance of winning. To be among the last few players time and time again had made me feel like I'd do people a favor if they just didn't need to pick me. I did not like soccer, so I thought that this ministry opportunity could not be from God.

I looked away to make up my mind about how I would respond to him. Politely, I was going to turn down this outreached hand. In all reality, I did not want to share the gospel through sports.

Then the Lord spoke to my heart. *Were you not looking for a ministry?*

Instantly, the Lord convicted me that this was the direction He wanted me to follow. Instead of turning down the offer, I asked for the phone number. Now excited that I had direction from the Lord, I could not wait to give them a call in the morning.

That next morning, I got into my car and called the phone number.

Someone answered. "Hello. Good morning."

"Yeah, hello. This is Stan. You don't know me, but I am getting in my car right now and would love to join for the event if you let me."

"Um … okay, come on down. We can always use help in one area or another."

Within weeks after the event, I was volunteering four days a week for this ministry called Agapē and their sports ministry, Athletes in Action. A few weeks later, I started volunteering full-time for the ministry team in Rotterdam. I was so full of gratitude to finally be around people who knew my Jesus, I did everything they would let me do: kids clubs, street evangelism, youth nights, maintenance, and sports ministry.

One night, after sharing what Jesus had done for a man like me with a predominantly Muslim audience, I closed the

door to our building. It was a cool, bright night, and while I
was in wonder about the way I had been able to testify that
day, I thought... *Maybe the Lord will have me lead a Bible
study at some point?* Seeing what Jesus was doing in me made
me consider that maybe, just maybe, God could do that?
I remember thinking that for the first time so clearly since
speaking in groups, let alone a large audience, had always been
close to impossible for me. My younger brother was always
the one who gave speeches at family events or celebrations,
not me. I had passionately despised every public speaking
opportunity that had ever come my way since I was a child. If
there was any way I could avoid speaking for a group, I would.
So, the idea of leading a Bible study was an out-of-this-world
kind of thought for me. It overwhelmed me to realize that
maybe it was possible for Jesus to pick me up and change me
around so much that He could use someone like me and my
voice to add to the lives of others.

CHAPTER 13

CRAZY DIRECTION

As happens to many who are drawn to the matters of the Kingdom, I began working hard at trying to serve and see people saved from their sins. Telling people about Jesus everywhere I went in addition to saying yes to every ministry that would accept my help began to take its toll.

I was working too hard, wrongly believing that if I could just explain accurately to people what had happened to me, and if I could get them to really listen, then anyone who would hear it and understand it would get saved. I worked as hard as I could, but I soon started to get tired from putting in so much effort and seeing so little fruit. A few months into my ministry work, I got offered a leadership position.

Accepting a leading role in one of the ministries meant making a commitment and giving up volunteering at other ministries. The Lord had told me to be in this place, but He had not said for how long. Making that commitment felt like I would lose my freedom to simply follow Him instantly once He would speak.

I had no witness in my heart and no clear answer from the Lord even though I sought Him for it. For a while, I was not giving my leaders an answer to the point where I felt like avoiding them. I did not even want to run into them. I felt like waiting on God was the right decision, but it seemed to me that no one else felt that was the best decision for my life.

Now, despite being finally in the midst of believers, I once again felt alone, just me and the Lord. I was so joyous to finally know Him, yet in a strange way it was painful to have God be the only one who could fully be close to me.

Around that same time, I had to make some other decisions. I still owned my company, but working on a volunteer basis full-time to spread the gospel had caused my company's income to slow down significantly. I made a simple plan to relocate my company to the city where the ministry was located and find myself a house with a garage so I could set up a workshop. One of my product lines called "kit boats" could be housed in the workshop. I would make enough money to continue as a volunteer at the ministry a few days a week and be able to cover my expenses. I wanted to use building the boats to teach a trade to some of the youth I worked with. I hoped that this would help them stay out of trouble, as some of them were growing up in rough neighborhoods. If possible, I wanted to help steer them toward a decent, stable job. In the meantime, working with them would provide a relational opportunity for me to share the gospel with them.

***

A friend and colleague from the ministry had assured me that I could stay with his parents while I looked for the right home in the city.

"Thank you for letting me stay here," I said.

His mom gave me a welcoming smile as we got ready for breakfast. I felt comfortable, like a part of a family, so welcome, loved, and wanted, but the Lord was about to throw me a curve ball.

That morning, it was bothering me again that I had no direction and no answer to give to my leadership regarding the position offered to me. I knew what it felt like to have clarity and direction from my Lord, and even though there were no real reasons I could come up with for me to say no to them, as strange as it was to me, I just didn't have that go-ahead-this-is-where-I'm-leading-you kind of peace.

While I was deep in thought about all of this at the breakfast table, my friend's mom brought up her nephew in conversation.

"He is in a ministry school in America. They learn teaching, preaching and discipleship. It's a ministry founded by David Wilkerson."

I had never heard of a David Wilkerson and had never been to America. I had sworn I would never live in any other country but my own, and I could not see myself even visiting the United States of America in my lifetime.

I believed I did not have the time to take off and go lock myself away in some Bible school for years. *People are going to hell because they don't know Jesus. I don't have time for something like that.*

On top of that, I remember so vividly what I had seen as a kid. The people who had gone to a Bible school were good people. *A school like that is for people who have their stuff together, people who do not really struggle and are kind, and they definitely don't have a background like mine. No, people who go to these schools are people who seek to do good with their lives. They have a good heart. Those people are bred in churches, and they allowed the Church environment to nourish, shape, and prune them into a Bible school kind of person. That is not me, not by a long shot.*

However, trying to be polite, I engaged her as she handed me a bookmark from that school. I was eating my peanut butter sandwich as I reached out for the bookmark. The moment I touched it, the Lord spoke instantly, powerfully, and clearly, *You have to go there!*

I almost choked on my sandwich. In that moment, so much happened. I overflowed with joy for the clear direction from the Lord. I felt so loved. He still cared about me despite the fact that I had struggled with pornography lately. *This is crazy.* A million questions started to come to mind … *A ministry school? Me? What …?*

I did not know that her nephew had given these bookmarks prayerfully to his aunt with specific instructions. He had told her, "Pray, and give these out, but only to somebody you really believe has to go here."

He and I had lived in the same town growing up. We were never in the same friend groups, but we knew of each other. Now that we both believed and trusted in the same Lord, our Lord called us to a reunion on the other side of the world in the same ministry school.

If that wasn't enough, the Lord's humor really shone through when I got home and excitedly told all this to my parents.

My mom told me, "I was in school with his mom."

In the Lord's letting me see this, I felt such a powerful confirmation of His love for me. The way God made me feel in this moment was amazing, as if He did all of this so I would feel loved and noticed by Him. Even more so, He made me feel that He desired to be noticed by me.

Just weeks later, the Lord woke me up at night and gave me clear instructions. *Stop your company. Don't worry about the customers. Don't worry about the money.*

As I obeyed the Lord and began to shut down my company, I just had to trust that God would deal with the consequences of my obedience. I had multiple customers who had already paid my company for projects that were not finished yet. I closed down the company, and as I held my breath to see how this would all turn out, I began to get the phone calls. In one week's time, every single one of my customers called me by their own initiative to let me know that they were canceling their project but that I could keep the money. Stunned by the orderly care and involvement of my Lord, I began to wholly focus on the next journey of obedience at hand—studying in the USA.

I still thank the Lord for speaking to me about Summit International School of Ministry. If He had not given me such a clear word, there was no way I could have done it. By the time I arrived at the school, I realized how tired my way of doing full-time ministry had made me in just eight months. The Lord had to teach me so much, mostly to just be saved, to just be loved by Him. During my time in the school, He started to squeeze a whole bunch of stuff out of me. He used the school in many ways in my life but constantly as a pressure cooker to prepare me in a deep, fast, and painful way for what was coming.

The rules, the structure, the culture, and the language in the school all made me feel like a foreigner in every aspect of life. They had me study and read a doctrine book while I just wanted to get started with learning more English words so I could understand people.

During school hours, I would focus with everything in me to try to catch the point of the class. The first weeks were very trying. I read the first page of my doctrine book several times, and I could not even get the gist of what it was about. I simply did not know the words or terminology. I had enough of a vocabulary to survive a holiday abroad, but that was about it. By the time I was ready to burn the doctrine book, I decided to put it down for a little while.

I failed my English class, cursed people out for messing with my laundry, and got called into the office on more than one occasion. But in this place, the healing power of the Lord kept cleaning my wounds, allowing them to continue to heal properly. The staff impacted me a lot, especially when I had rebellion come up inside of me and chose to break rules (sometimes deliberately). The leadership always had grace for me; they never seemed disappointed in me. I had never known that kind of treatment.

Then, when I would be doing well but made an honest mistake there would be some real consequences, and to my surprise, it helped me grow every time. People had never consistently treated me that way. I never felt like an inconvenience to the staff, even when I was pushing it. They made me feel like I was more than worth the investment. It was the love of God inside them and through them that kept changing me one degree at a time.

***

In the first months, as the Lord began the process of slowing me down and teaching me how to just be, I started to realize how hard it was for me that everyone around me had already been saved right there in the school. I had no one to share the gospel with, no one who had not heard about my Lord. I felt useless, miserable, and guilty at times. I had the belief that my effort could and should contribute to the saving of people, but the Lord was taking me on a journey to learn to look to Him all the time, and to fully expect Him to show up in all things.

To follow Him, I began learning to simply obey His leading. To learn to be content with being a follower of Jesus, I began to listen. In my mind, I looked back over my shoulder and started to see a trail of Kingdom fruit sprouting up. I became quieter and did less, yet I saw more and more fruit come up as I learned to wait and follow. I learned to stop trying to do the work of Jesus. That was what had gotten me so tired in such a short time in the ministry. It was a hard but necessary lesson and time of being shaped to learn to just do my part in obedience and to leave the job of the Spirit of Christ to the Spirit of Christ.

The quietness and patience of trust was being worked into me in that place. As that work was being done by the Spirit of God, slowly I became still enough for God to begin addressing things in me that needed His gospel and His touch. I was so focused on other people needing Jesus that God had to shut my life down for two years in this Bible school so I would let God in. I had never learned yet to let Him into the deep places, the places we don't talk about.

CHAPTER 14

HEALING FROM ABORTION

Sometimes I share and explain that Jesus saves, despite what kind of sins you are in and despite the depth of the darkness in your past. I'll say something like, "I would know, with my past, that there is nothing that Jesus cannot save and heal you from! I am one of the worst sinners. I have committed the worst sins, and yet He did it, even for me. He will do it for you as well!"

At times I get the reply, "Well, it can't be that bad. You didn't kill anybody right?" I usually hear this when a well-meaning person mistakenly thinks that I'm being too hard on myself or that I may be putting myself down due to broken self-esteem and they are seeking to pull me out of a pit they imagine I am in.

***

For years, even though I spoke about it, I did not realize how deep the pain and guilt had gripped me. I believed I was forgiven, and I did feel forgiven by Jesus, but there was something that remained a part of me. In my emotions and actions, there was still clear evidence from time to time that something was deeply unhealed.

For what felt like a long time, I played that off by just referencing the severity of the sins. It was easy to justify the pain and the way I carried it by saying, "I know what I know, and I can remember the things I have done. I cannot unknow them, and it weighs heavy to carry my kind of memories." I genuinely believed that it made sense that this was just how it was for someone who had done such unspeakable things. But God had different plans. Beyond forgiveness, He wanted to heal me—truly heal me.

While in Bible school, I loved spending time at Roosters, the coffee shop on the campus. The open fireplace always set a great atmosphere, and I loved spending time with my friends there. We would talk about the Lord, play games, or just discuss everyday life. But one time, the Lord had something very different in mind. I was clueless, sitting there in the coffee shop.

I had these moments from time to time when my emotions would flare up. The only way I can describe it is that I would feel this epic kind of loneliness, a very specific and strange kind. It made me feel as if I had survived something that no one else I knew had been through, like there were painful scars that told stories that no one could relate to. It made me isolate certain parts of my emotional self; in doing so, I was robbing the people around me and myself from true intimate friendships, the kind God wants to give us in one another. The excuse I used, or a part of it, was the Lord. I thought, *He understands. I will just be alone with Him since no one else around me can relate. The Lord was there when it happened, and He knows the pain I carry.*

These moments boiled up in me because of abortion in my blackened past. Everyone knew the testimony of what Jesus had taken me out of and forgiven me for, but knowing the things I knew and having been a part of the sins that embody the character of Satan, there was this unique kind of loneliness. It had given birth to an attitude that said, "I have been forgiven, but people do not know what it is like to be forgiven for such things."

I would feel some of the pain and responsibility, not being able to completely forgive myself as Jesus had done, not being able to let Him take full responsibility for my life and my sins. I would sit alone and think, process, just me and the Lord, no one else.

Friends came and went this time as I was going through it sitting at Roosters. I tried to interpret their looks and imagine their thoughts as I saw that people were giving me my space. I figured that they realized I was feeling the heaviness. They had seen it in me before, and they knew I had to be alone with the Lord.

As I sat alone at a table, responsibly mourning over the past, the Holy Spirit out of nowhere spoke to my heart and to my understanding, clearly and powerfully. *You do not want the cross in this area of your life. You do not want it to be finished. You love the pain.*

I was shocked, but now suddenly I could see. It was true! I loved carrying around this pain. It ensured that I had something that gave people a reason to feel compassion and care for me. I was selfishly comforted knowing that people felt like I was a special case. Holding onto the pain and the guilt made me live in a way that reminded the people around me of the pain and not the healer. In this, it guaranteed me their continued compassion.

But then, as I was experiencing the conviction, I said in my heart, *No! I want the cross, I am so sorry Lord.*

And right away, the Spirit of God started to give me instructions, *"Grab a pen and paper and write a letter to your unborn child."*

Again, I was shocked. It shook me to my core. Breathing became harder as I scrambled up a piece of paper and started writing. From the very moment my pen hit the paper, the tears began to flow. I wrote about everything that had happened, apologizing, taking responsibility and speaking for the first time to this little one I had abandoned. I wept my heart out, and the tears turned into words as my pen kept writing.

Finally, as I finished the letter, I wanted to move my teary eyes back to the first words to read it over. Before I could start reading the opening words, and I so wanted to read it over, the Lord spoke to me again. *No! Walk to the fireplace and give it to me.*

Now weeping uncontrollably, I got up and walked toward the fire. Every step felt like my heart was being torn out. I don't know how long I stood before that fireplace, emotions I cannot describe in words and all the pain and guilt I had carried for years now transferred to a piece of paper. It was one of the hardest decisions of obedience and trust that the Lord had ever placed before me. The flames seemed to move in slow motion through my tears. Then finally, I let go and the fire took it all.

I still visit that fireplace from time to time; right there, the Lord did one of the greatest miracles in my life. I got healed. Right there, it was finally finished.

The Lord is not afraid or offended by the worst of your sins. There is no sin invented in hell dark enough that it has become taboo to Him. Jesus desperately wants to heal you on every level. He wants to move you forward into a life untainted and undefined by sin. He wants to give you a new life.

Yes, come into the light. Yes, don't let the truth be hidden. Yes, confess your sins to one another that you may be healed. Do these things, absolutely. But if you do these things as you trust Jesus, expect the Holy Spirit to show up to perform surgery on your soul.

He will lovingly tailor your journey of healing to the depth and severity of the pain you carry. Do not hold on. Don't decide on what you want to stay responsible for and what you are willing to be forgiven for. It is finished. Let Him take it and let Him show you His care and healing power.

If you let Him, He will.

CHAPTER 15

INNA

When I arrived on campus our first year, it was not long before I heard about the bubble effect. It was an intriguing thought that someone who would never have been on my radar would become someone that I would take note of once I started living on campus full-time. Despite the warnings, people began liking one another left and right. I did not expect to fall prey to this, but I ended up being no exception.

A memory came back so clearly right after registration. I remembered the prayer I prayed only a couple weeks after being saved: "I don't want to get married unless I can serve You better with her than without her."

Recently saved, I was looking toward finding a believing mate. However, I felt that she would need a similar past so she could understand me and relate to me. Feeling the call of God on my life as well made it, in my calculations, even more impossible to find the "right" one. To top it off, I could not imagine how I could ever have a marriage relationship that would include sex now that I was saved, forgiven, changed. Any thought of the sexual relationship that comes with marriage made me feel discomfort and resistant. Since the only sexual experiences I knew were dark and sinful, my feelings believed this area was corrupted by Satan, and I wanted no part of it. I genuinely felt it was better to stay far away from all that.

Despite all of this, a part of me was still behaving as if I had to find her, as if I had the ability to find that kind of a person who was a tailored fit for my life. I just could not stop looking for her. There was almost always a girl who had some level of my interest, if not a lot of it.

Somewhere deep down, I still believed that this right girl would fill up something I was feeling inside. I believed that I would feel more emotionally whole with the right girl. It was my selfish nature that also believed the give-and-take theory. I could not see it but was unwilling to be fulfilled in Christ alone. I was unwilling to be fully complete in Him, unwilling to become a whole person who is able to give without demanding something back, a person able to wait and love despite the other person's response or lack thereof.

The Lord wanted to teach me that love does not demand a response. He wanted to heal me into a place where I would finally be able to start giving love without putting any condition on it or demanding a response to it. That was how I had been living and misunderstanding it. If my so-called love went unanswered, I withdrew and moved on to someone who may answer to it in the way I liked and the way that pleased me. The Lord wanted to teach me that unless I removed all conditions, my love could not become a precious gift that had the power to change someone.

When I experienced feelings for someone, believing that may be the person I could really talk to, who could make me happy, complete me, and support my call, I used to call that feeling of being drawn to that person "love." When I felt attracted to a person because of what life could look like with her as opposed to without her, I thought I felt love. Nothing could have been further from the truth. I believed I would get something I desperately wanted out of the relationship with that person. Though they were "Christian" desires, the motivation was selfish, and if unmet, the feelings would cool down quickly. When I saw someone else whom I believed would meet those needs, the same feelings would flare up for this new person.

Time after time, if the attraction became mutual, it was always with someone who was looking for a similar deal, the give-and-take deal, the conditional one. It was most likely subconscious, but nevertheless, rooted in selfishness. God was going to teach me love. Love gives, no matter what the response. Love never shows up to take something or demand something. I had never loved a woman before.

After a while and some wakeup calls, I realized the challenge at hand. I was a flirt. One of the biggest lightbulbs that went off was the realization that I talked differently with a guy friend than with a female friend, even when I had no romantic interest in her. I began to realize there were many things, especially deeper emotional topics, that I preferred talking about with a female than with one of my male friends. I began to realize I was always looking for an emotional connection for myself in a boy-girl relationship whether I had romantic intentions or not.

I believed that I needed a woman to fill an emotional need I was experiencing. As logical as that may sound in today's world, it was all born out of that selfish desire. The flirtatious fruits that provoked untimely and unhealthy emotional bonds proved it!

I did not know or believe that a complete and healed person communicates with men and women on the same level, in the same ways, while having the same experience. I thought it normal that my conversations, the topics, and vulnerability felt deeper when I was conversing with a female friend compared to conversing with my guy friends. I loved that deep feeling, so I was open to experience it when the opportunity presented itself. It literally was as if each group served a different purpose in my life to fill different aspects of my emotional needs.

Call it European; call it "I am just more comfortable talking to girls"; call it what you want. The truth was witnessed to by the fruit, and I was not a safe place for girls at all. Deep down, the subconscious, selfish motives always caused me to end up with an unhealthy, unbalanced emotional connection.

During summer break between my first and second year in Summit International School of Ministry, one of my closest friends said it best: "Stan, you love the Lord and have really changed a lot, but in this area you have rotten fruit in your life."

This statement from a loving friend hit me hard. That moment truly marked the beginning of a deep change the Lord would begin to make.

***

The Holy Spirit kept placing those words heavily on my mind. The conviction kept growing, and my strength and goodwill trying to do better kept failing until eventually I prayed, "Lord would You make me a safe place for women? Amen."

It felt impossible that beyond my words and actions, even my emotions and feelings could and would change. Considering where the Lord had taken me from, I thought it ironic that I was asking for this kind of miracle; for someone with my past to become a safe place.

The Lord heard that prayer of surrender as I kept asking continuously. As a matter of fact, knowing Him, He probably caused all the pressure that squeezed that prayer out of me in the first place. I couldn't tell how He got it all done, but that same year a few weeks before Christmas break, I realized it.

One morning as I got out of bed, before doing anything, it hit me, almost in the same way as a revelation does. *It does not happen anymore. I have not felt that drive to look for that girl, for a good wife. I have not triggered anyone lately. It is gone. I am at peace.*

Then, Christmas break came around.

***

Three of us students went to Portland, Oregon, for different reasons. For one of my friends, Portland was simply home. For me, it was a cheaper option than flying back home to the Netherlands. It was just too expensive. When my classmate invited me, I was glad to spend Christmas around him and his family.

The first Sunday in Portland, my classmate was sharing the gospel at his parents' home church. At the beginning of the service, sitting in the front row, I looked around to see where his parents were sitting. I couldn't find them. I glanced over my right shoulder one more time and didn't see them. There must have been over five hundred people in the sanctuary. As I turned my head slowly back to the front while scanning the crowd, my life took a crazy turn. I glanced over this girl. I was not looking at her. We didn't even lock eyes. She was just in the path of my view like many others, but the moment she was in my line of sight the Holy Spirit spoke.

That is going to be your wife.

It was such an unexpected gut punch that I blurted out a cuss word in church.

Trying to regain my composure and figure out what in the world had just happened, I ended up not catching anything of the message that was preached. The whole time I was talking quietly to God. *Lord, You just set me free. I am finally content. You have me in a school where they ask us to lay down actively pursuing relationships so we can focus on You. God, You knew that before you sent me there! Why in the world would you tell me this?!*

Still arguing in my head with the Lord about His methods, I realized the service was over. We all got up, and people turned toward one another to catch up and shake hands. I did not know anyone except the other students from my school, so after just a few hands I ran out of people. I was just starting to feel like an outsider when, from the corner of my eye, I saw her. My jaw dropped.

She is making her way here. No, she can't be. What am I going to say? There is no way. Wait, what if the Lord told her too?

She introduced herself. "Hi, nice to meet you guys."

I could see her lips still moving, her hand reaching out to shake mine. It was as if I were completely zoned out, in shock. I could not follow her words and was just looking at her.

Then everything came back into focus. She was talking with another student now. It did not seem like the Lord had told her. As she was talking with another friend of mine about the Lord and school, I just tried to process all of this.

Lord, we are here in Portland for less than three weeks. I am not to pursue a relationship. How? Why? What was her name … Inna?

While we made our way out of the sanctuary, my friend asked me what I thought of service.

I replied, "By the grace of God, you're going to see me end up with this Inna girl!"

He responded, "Bro … that's crazy …" Then he looked around and ran off.

No, no, no, no, no, he is not! Before I could do anything, he had caught up to her. *They know each other?* I joined them, expecting the worst. By the time we left the church, he had set up a midweek snowboarding day trip with a bunch of friends, including Inna.

***

You know the spark? Yeah, we didn't have that. There was no flirting, and no obvious interest. There was just nothing. I was very intrigued because of what the Lord had said, but she was not necessarily my type. I wasn't her type either, and as much as I tried to join in the conversation, there was no stirring between us. It was not flowing. It was more awkward than anything, but I believed the Lord.

The first time we ever had a one-on-one conversation was during the drive to Mount Hood to go on that snowboarding day trip. It was just Inna, her brother, her cousin, and me. Everyone else, including the guys from my school, had bailed out. At the last minute, her brother and cousin decided to take their own car so they could stay behind longer.

So, there she was, alone in the car with what felt to her like a stranger. We had a good drive up. We talked about the Lord, and other than that had mostly surface-level conversations. After an hour-and-a-half drive, we got to the mountain. I had imagined that we would be enjoying this day around one another, that every time we would end up back at the bottom, we would get in the ski lift and have an opportunity to make all kinds of conversation. In my imagination, I would begin to get to know her today little by little.

I was wrong! The moment she locked the car, pointed everything out, and told me what time we had to be back to leave, she was gone. I did not see her again until the time we had to meet up to drive home. We made our way back to the vehicle while I thought to myself, *This day went really differently from how I thought it would.*

Back in the car, as we pulled out of the parking lot, she asked me, "So, how did you get to Summit International School of Ministry?"

About to start the hour-and-a-half drive home, I quickly and silently prayed, *Lord I believe You. If You are giving me this girl, You're going to have to be the one to do it all. I know the life You are leading me into, and I need a special woman, wholly dedicated to You and Your plan. Lord, I will not do anything to make her like me, and I cannot have her feel like I first developed a friendship, then once we felt our relationship could handle it, I would drop my whole testimony on her. Lord, she will know all things before this will even be a friendship. She will never have to wonder about anything—never. Amen.*

Starting at the very beginning, I shared my entire journey. I told her everything I had done, and all the Lord had done. It was not long before her body language made it unmistakably clear that she was not interested in me whatsoever. She loved what the Lord had done, but nothing was clearer than that she was closed off to me.

**

Over the next two weeks, we spoke about the Lord a lot, sometimes in groups and sometimes just the two of us over a cup of coffee.

Toward the end of my stay in town, I told her, "I like you, and I would like to meet your parents."

She told me, "Well, I don't like you, and nobody is meeting anybody."

Even though it was not by Inna's choice, I did get to meet her parents before leaving town; twice, and she was not happy.

Before leaving, I told her, "We are not really going to have contact while I am in school, but if this is from the Lord, He will tell you. He will speak to you."

Then, the guys and I flew back to school.

**

During my last semester, I was going to learn a lot about what love is, and what it is not. It was not long before Inna completely cut off the little communication that we did have. I received no more responses when I left a message; no calls, nothing. Just like when I was around her in Portland, there was no spark.

All kinds of insecurities and fears were coming up in me and raging through my feelings and my emotions during these months. Even some of my friends began to advise me to let this go, seeing how hard it was on me to have nothing to hold on to but what the Lord had clearly said to me.

There were no confirming actions or words from Inna; no "I like you too," no initiative at all from her side. Despite it all, I just had to decide, and I made up my mind that I was going to love her whether she would ever know it or not. I trusted that the Lord would see my heart and that He would keep His word to me.

I realized that I would rather wait before the Lord and keep my heart for Inna than to ever move on toward someone else. I could not reach her. I couldn't do anything but sit, preserve my heart, and trust the Lord.

This was the first time I decided to love someone even though there was no guarantee that I would ever get anything out of it. As a matter of fact, I didn't even have a guarantee that she would ever know that I was making these lifetime decisions for her in my heart. Even though it was just me and the Lord there in the room, it was one of the most deep, vulnerable, intimidating, and scary decisions I had ever committed myself to.

Then the Lord revealed to me—*Now that you know what love is, you can perfectly love Inna in obedience to me. That's what I want to give her through you, whether or not she will respond to you. I will give you peace and satisfaction, and fill you so you can do this.*

Overwhelmed by the incredible revelation that according to God's opinion and against all odds, with all I had ever done and failed to do, I had love for a daughter of the King in my heart. My thoughts were racing. I wanted to share, but the Lord put a stop to it right then and there. He told me, *Do not tell her you love her.*

Months later, I would learn that the Lord had spoken to Inna four different times in four different ways, telling her that I was the man He wanted to give to her. There was a reason the Lord had to confirm that four times to her—she really did not like me.

Eventually, on not much more than simple obedience, Inna flew in with her cousin Iryna for my graduation. As I sat on the stage, I saw her walk in, barely making it on time. Pure, ecstatic joy filled my heart. I did not know the Lord had spoken to her four times in the months of separation, and I had still not told anyone else that the Lord had spoken to me about her.

That evening, I told her, "I want to get to know you better, but only as my girlfriend." Two weeks later, we were engaged, and before the end of the year, we got married.

By that time, she liked me.

***

Since then, we have been inseparable in every way. We received full-time, live-in internship and mentorship from pastors Glen and Mona Stephen in Canada. We have lived in four different countries and moved over twenty times as the Lord has led us to spread the gospel and make disciples for Christ together. We have founded and supported various ministries and churches, including Safe House Ministries and Safe House Church in Portland, Oregon.

We have received our precious children from the Lord. We see Him save sinners, time and time again, making Himself known, bringing hope to people in the worst situations.

We have never seen the Lord fail anyone who trusted Him at His word, and we continue to believe and see that Jesus is preparing His bride, getting her ready for His soon return.

I no longer have just my journey with the Lord. We have our journey with Him, personal yet in unity, together serving the Lord. God gave me a helper in Inna. Everything God started in me when He and I got to know each other is now being helped forward. He is a giving God of grace to the tenth power. God gave me Inna, a heavenly fit, tailor-made, no expense spared, for a man like me. God redeems, restores, and orchestrates.

Trust Him. He does not fail.

CHAPTER 16

BETWEEN YOU AND ME

Now you know! Jesus Christ has loved someone like me, someone who used to be stuck in lies and bondage, living like a male prostitute, destroying people's lives. He has taken me, with all that I was and ever failed to be, and He picked me up. He saved me, cleansed me, strengthened me, gave me a mate and children, and sent me out.

Beyond sending me out for kingdom purposes, He is close to me. He treats me like the love of His life. The way He treats me changes me still, every single day. I will never be able to describe what it does to me, knowing what I came from and still seeing undeniably the God of all creation love me and give me His undivided attention; but I know someone who can show you, someone who wants to show you. I know someone who loves you more than you realize today. He is willing to do for you above and beyond what He has done for me. When you begin to trust Him and His word in the smallest of ways, He will show up for you and take your hand, one step at a time. To Him, you are worth it more than a thousand times over, but don't take it from me. Find out for yourself. He is willing to show you.

Because of the cross of Jesus Christ, there is nothing that the devil, you, or anyone else can bring to the table to ever change God's mind about you. He loves you.

On the cross, Jesus cried out with you and me in mind, *"It is finished!"*

He marked the unshakable truth that there is nothing left that could ever get in between Himself and you. I challenge you to believe this gospel, and you will see God begin to do relationship with you. You will see Him keep His promises to you—yes to you—despite your past, present, or Satan's evil plans. That is the power of the cross, the perfect cross that God the Father wanted available for you.

"For God did not send His Son into the world to condemn the world, but that the world through Him might be saved" (John 3:17 NKJV).

***

If you feel stuck in any area of life, if you have dirty stains on your soul, you need to know! God has never, and will never, look away from you in disgust.

The Father is not seeking to reject you for your failures and your sin. He wants you to look up toward Him with the eyes of your heart and see the truth. It takes courage to find out if He would surround you, save you, and heal you into a testimony to the risen Lord. To feel like all you have is reason to be rejected by God yet to decide to come to Him because there is a cross requires faith.

God wants you to stop trying to work at removing your sins in your own strength. All you will ever have in your favor before the Father will be the cross of Jesus Christ. The Father wants you to find out and see clearly with the eyes of your heart that the cross is abundantly more than enough payment for Him. He wants you to see in His eyes what Jesus has done for you!

If you are a sinner, you qualify. Expect Him to show up.

God, in His love and gentleness, called me out of darkness with a voice of urgency. As I, with the tiniest bit of trust, looked toward Him, He lifted me out of my darkness. He healed and restored, He called and equipped, and every breath

I take and word I speak is a testimony against the powers of death and darkness.

It is impossible that someone like me has written this book. It is impossible that I know Him. It is impossible that I have not relapsed into my old life. I know the dark powers, and I know myself, but now I know Jesus. It's impossible, yet here I am, free and rejoicing!

That is what the cross has done and what the cross will do for you.

The longer I am saved, the simpler things become. I know the one thing I was really good at was sin, and I know how God behaves toward me in spite of it.

All I can do is point to the cross. That's His reason.

***

The Lord has a unique, special calling on your life, a tailored purpose. One of the questions we hear often is, "How do I know I have a calling, and if I do, how do I know what it is?"

Wanting clear, simple understanding, I took that question to prayer until I got an answer. This was what the Lord told me: *Everyone who receives the promised Holy Spirit is called, because there is a calling on the Spirit of Christ. As they walk with Me and know Me, I will tell them what it is.*

If you are sick of your sin, willing to turn from it, and you believe today that Jesus is the Son of God, then that makes you a believer. Believing that Jesus is the Son of God means for you personally that you are forgiven before God, perfectly clean before the Father. All your sins are paid for by the sacrifice of Jesus on the cross.

If you believe Him at His word, then He will send you His Holy Spirit. He will come to you in a way that can enable anyone who repents and believes to become an effective vessel.

If you surrender to Him and trust Him, there is unlimited potential as to how much damage the Lord will do through you to Satan's war plan over people's lives. In your trusting obedience, you will see the Lord starting to push out the darkness and the powers that keep people around you bound, blind, and enslaved.

You are called to be a vessel. Different purposes and positions are undoubtedly divided within the Kingdom of God; however, every part will somehow play an important role in seeing the lost get saved, the eyes of the blind opened, liberty proclaimed, accompanied by the setting free of those in bondage.

God is still on a mission to save the lost and to get the saved ready for His return. Please do not ever downplay the part that you are called to and entrusted with in His kingdom. God is calling us to active duty. Look at who your God is. Know Him, and let it be known that Christ has come. It is finished.

When you will pray and trust Him, when you will wholly surrender, there is no telling what God may do in our generation.

He has taken me from prostitution to preaching. Have you asked lately: *God, where are you taking me?*

SCAN HERE

www.stanmons.com

Connect with Pastor Stan

Reach out to Safe House Church

Find more resources

ORDER INFORMATION

To order individual copies go to
redemption-press.com/bookstore

For discounts on bulk orders
send an email to
bookorders@redemption-press.com.
subject: bulk orders

www.ingramcontent.com/pod-product-compliance
Lightning Source LLC
Chambersburg PA
CBHW021110231025
34293CB00003B/13